D. H. LAWRENCE Poems selected by TOM PAULIN

David Herbert Lawrence was born in Nottinghamshire in 1885. Predominantly remembered as a novelist, Lawrence began writing poetry when he was nineteen and published his first pieces in 1909 in the *English Review*. His first book of verse, *Love Poems and Others*, appeared in 1913. This was followed by *Amores* (1916), *Look! We Have Come Through* (1917), *New Poems* (1918), *Bay* (1919), *Tortoises* (1921), *Birds, Beasts and Flowers* (1923) and *Pansies* (1929). His *Collected Poems* appeared in 1928 and *Last Poems* was published posthumously in 1932. D. H. Lawrence died of tuberculosis in Vence, France, in 1930.

Tom Paulin was born in Leeds in 1949 but grew up in Belfast, and was educated at the universities of Hull and Oxford. He has published eight collections of poetry as well as a *Selected Poems 1972–1990*, two major anthologies, two versions of Greek drama and several critical works, including *The Day-Star of Liberty: William Hazlitt's Radical Style* and, most recently, *Crusoe's Secret: The Aesthetics of Dissent*. His most recent collection of poems is *The Road to Inver* (2004). Well known for his appearances on the BBC's *Late Review*, he is also the G. M. Young Lecturer in English Literature at Hertford College, Oxford.

D. H. LAWRENCE

Poems selected by TOM PAULIN

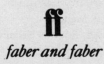

faber and faber

First published in 2007
by Faber and Faber Limited
3 Queen Square London WC1N 3AU

Photoset by RefineCatch Ltd, Bungay, Suffolk
Printed in England by Bookmarque Ltd, Croydon

A CIP record for this book
is available from the British Library

ISBN 978–0–571–23491–2

10 9 8 7 6 5 4 3 2 1

Contents

Introduction

> Man fixes some wonderful erection of his own between
> himself and the wild chaos, and gradually goes bleached and
> stifled under his parasol. Then comes a poet, enemy of
> convention, and makes a slit in the umbrella; and lo! the
> glimpse of chaos is a vision, a window to the sun.
>
>   – D.H. Lawrence, 'Chaos in Poetry'

To offer a selection of Lawrence's poems is to present a critical
reading of the nearly one thousand pages of the *Collected
Poems*. It is to watch the journey he made from being a compe-
tent Georgian poet who rhymed easily, but not especially com-
fortably, to becoming, next to his hero Whitman, one of the
greatest masters of free verse in the language. To participate in
that journey towards the slit in the conventional umbrella one
has to notice how the early 'Dream-Confused' begins with a
confident series of questions:

> Is that the moon
> At the window so big and red?
> No-one in the room?
> No-one near the bed?

Then Lawrence loses energy:

> Listen, her shoon
> Palpitating down the stair!
> – Or a beat of wings at the window there?

The archaic 'shoon' and the arguably obtrusive 'palpitating' pull
the poem into a conventional frame.

    What Lawrence is drawn to is process, something he calls 'active
sheen', and we can see this in the early 'The Wild Common':

> Rabbits, handfuls of brown earth lie
> Low-rounded on the mournful turf they have bitten down
>   to the quick.

Are they asleep? – are they living? – Now see, when I
Lift my arms, the hill bursts and heaves under their
    spurting kick!

That 'spurting kick' and all that 'quick' means in English are his real subject, but it took him years to gain the confidence to approach it in a voice that is recognizably Lawrence's. Jackson Pollock once said, 'I don't paint nature, I am nature,' and Lawrence, following a similarly puritan aesthetic of apparently chaotic extremity, had to reject rhyme and become nature in order to write his finest poems.

We can attend to the beginnings of this identification with process, with things happening now, in 'End of Another Home Holiday':

Ah home, suddenly I love you
As I hear the sharp clean trot of a pony down the road,
Succeeding sharp little sounds dropping into silence
Clear upon the long-drawn hoarseness of a train across the
    valley.

Later, he describes a 'wild young heifer, glancing distraught, With a strange new knocking of life at her side'. Lawrence is still hearing the pony's sharp clean trot – it's there in 'knocking' – in the sequence of sounds he hears many years later in New Mexico:

Trot-trot to the mottled foot-hills, cedar-mottled and piñon,
Did you ever see an otter?
Silvery-sided, fish-fanged, fierce-faced, whiskered, mottled.

When I trot my little pony through the aspen-trees of the
    canyon,
Behold me trotting at ease betwixt the slopes of the golden
Great and glistening-feathered legs of the horse of Horus.

What we catch here in 'Autumn at Taos' is Lawrence's confidence in that trotting pattern of sound, a pattern which gives great emphasis to that final adjective 'mottled', a sound repeated in the next stanza and later in the 'fish-dotted foothills', the 'otter's whisker' and the 'squatting Rockies.'

With this fascination with sound as process goes an interest in 'plasm', an unusual, because scientific, word for a Georgian poet to use. In 'Corot', a workmanlike early poem, he says that

The grey, plasm-limpid, pellucid advance
Of the luminous purpose of Life stands out.

He uses the term again in a poem not included in this selection, 'Embankment at Night, before the War', where he rhymes 'chasm' with 'intertwined plasm'. He wants his poems to be close to the quick, but one finds in the early poems so many limp cadences, flaccid rhythms and too-obvious, somehow null subjects, that the breakthrough seems endlessly postponed.

The discovery of his sure-grained personal voice comes with 'Piano', a poem which stands out, partly because Lawrence revised and rewrote it. The original poem is good in its own right:

Somewhere beneath that piano's superb sleek black
Must hide my mother's piano, little and brown, with the back
That stood close to the wall, and the front's faded silk, both
    torn,
And the keys with little hollows, that my mother's fingers
    had worn.

Softly, in the shadows, a woman is singing to me
Quietly, through the years I have crept back to see
A child sitting under the piano, in the boom of the shaking
    strings
Pressing the little poised feet of the mother who smiles as
    she sings.

The full throated woman has chosen a winning, living song
And surely the heart that is in me must belong
To the old Sunday evenings, when darkness wandered outside
And hymns gleamed on our warm lips, as we watched
    mother's fingers glide.

Or this is my sister at home in the old front room
Singing love's first surprised gladness, alone in the gloom.
She will start when she sees me, and blushing, spread out
    her hands
To cover my mouth's raillery, till I'm bound in her shame's
    heart-spun bands.

A woman is singing me a wild Hungarian air
And her arms, and her bosom, and the whole of her soul is
    bare,
And the great black piano is clamouring as my mother's
    never could clamour
And my mother's tunes are devoured of this music's
    ravaging glamour.

Once again it is a process of changing sounds which draws
Lawrence in and makes him write one of his most accomplished early poems.

Lawrence begins his revision with the second stanza, which he rewrites (see page 23). Note how he changes 'little' to 'small', so it gives more force to 'smiles', making the line pause slightly, and note also how the piano's *p* sound is repeated in 'pressing' and 'poised'. Like the clean sharp trot of the pony, the three strong stresses on 'small, poised feet' run against the iambic and anapaestic rhythms. But 'Piano' is a one-off, his only really successful rhyming poem, and one which stands tall among the nearly two hundred pages of early poems. It's only right at the end of his rhyming poems that we find in the last two poems – 'Disagreeable Advice' and 'Restlessness' – the beginnings of a new rhythm he is going to trust and go with.

'Disagreeable Advice' begins:

Always, sweetheart,
Carry into your room the blossoming boughs of cherry,
Almond and apple and pear diffuse with light, that very
Soon strews itself on the floor; and keep the radiance of spring
Fresh quivering.

With its short opening line – direct and spoken – and the enjambement of the third line this is more like free verse. Then we find a triumphant announcement in prose of the new, free style, the rent in the umbrella. Lawrence's introduction to the 1918 American edition of his poems is one of his most important pieces of critical prose, which is why I have included 'Poetry of the Present' as an appendix.

Lawrence begins by dividing poetry into two categories – the poetry of the 'far future, exquisite and ethereal', and the poetry of the past, 'rich, magnificent'. In the opening paragraphs of the introduction he rejects: 'Perfected bygone moments, perfected moments in the glimmering futurity, these are the treasured gem-like lyrics of Shelley and Keats.' He then offers another kind of poetry: 'the poetry of that which is at hand: the immediate present', and states that with this poetry there is 'no plasmic finality, nothing crystal, permanent'. Here we look at 'the very white quick of nascent creation'. His prose is less that of a conventional introduction, more a type of paean or prose poem to the poetry of the present:

> Give me nothing fixed, set, static. Don't give me the infinite or the eternal: nothing of infinity, nothing of eternity. Give me the still, white seething, the incandescence and the coldness of the incarnate moment: the moment, the quick of all change and haste and opposition: the moment, the immediate present, the Now.

Here he shifts his metaphor for the poetry of the 'immediate present' from biology – plasm – to imagery drawn from industrialism – steel foundries – and so contradicts much of what he elsewhere says in opposition to factories and city life.

He then shifts the metaphor back to nature: 'this is the unrestful, ungraspable poetry of the sheer present, poetry whose very permanency lies in its wind-like transit. Whitman's is the best poetry of this kind.' Free verse, he states, 'has its own *nature* . . . is neither star nor pearl, but instantaneous like plasm'.

We can see this free-verse aesthetic at work in his most famous and most successful poem 'Snake', where the snake Lawrence is observing in the hot garden of his rented villa in Taormina

> slowly, very slowly, as if thrice adream,
> Proceeded to draw his slow length curving round
> And climb again the broken bank of my wall-face.

Here, Lawrence cunningly alludes to Pope's criticism of obvious rhymed verse:

> A needless alexandrine ends the song
> That like a wounded snake drags its slow length along.

For a moment, the snake has become a natural symbol of rhymed verse's perfected bygone moments – as it moves it appears to break out into free verse, which is never static in Lawrence's formulation, even though the line 'And climb again the broken bank of my wall-face' is a particularly subtle alexandrine – it has six feet and deftly manages the inevitable, often obtrusive, caesura after 'bank'.

We can see how Lawrence draws on conventional verse for his best moments in 'Bare Fig Trees', which begins in a deliberately strained manner:

> Fig-trees, weird fig-trees
> Made of thick smooth silver,
> Made of sweet, untarnished silver in the sea-southern air –
> I say untarnished, but I mean opaque –

The first three lines, weighed down by adjectives, are failing to get off the ground, then Lawrence throws in an interjection, which is a perfect and spontaneous iambic pentameter – 'I say untarnished, but I mean opaque'. This is the poetry of the present or what Lawrence in the introduction to the American edition of his poems calls 'the insurgent naked throb of the instant moment', the 'very white quick of nascent creation'. It demonstrates that free verse can call on traditional iambic verse without offering a perrfected, bygone moment – instead this iambic line is a moment of living chaos, of sudden inspiration, in which we hear Lawrence's apparently unregulated voice.

Although the poems that make up the last four hundred pages of the *Collected Poems* are, it has to be said, largely failures, Lawrence faced his imminent and painful death in the short, beautiful 'Bavarian Gentians', which begins with another run of slow-paced adjectives:

> Not every man has gentians in his house
> In soft September, at slow, sad Michaelmas.

The lines get longer and longer as Lawrence holds on to life and imagines being

> enfolded in the deeper dark
> of the arms Plutonic, and pierced with the passion of dense
>   gloom,
> among the splendour of torches in darkness, shedding
>   darkness on the lost bride and her groom.

He imagines being united with Persephone in a moment that is as moving as the recollected, musical present of his childhood in 'Piano'.

TOM PAULIN

D. H. LAWRENCE

The Wild Common

The quick sparks on the gorse-bushes are leaping
Little jets of sunlight texture imitating flame;
Above them, exultant, the peewits are sweeping:
They have triumphed again o'er the ages, their screamings
    proclaim.

Rabbits, handfuls of brown earth, lie
Low-rounded on the mournful turf they have bitten down to
    the quick.
Are they asleep? – are they living? – Now see, when I
Lift my arms, the hill bursts and heaves under their spurting
    kick!

The common flaunts bravely; but below, from the rushes
Crowds of glittering king-cups surge to challenge the
    blossoming bushes;
There the lazy streamlet pushes
His bent course mildly; here wakes again, leaps, laughs, and
    gushes

Into a deep pond, an old sheep-dip,
Dark, overgrown with willows, cool, with the brook ebbing
    through so slow;
Naked on the steep, soft lip
Of the turf I stand watching my own white shadow quivering
    to and fro.

What if the gorse-flowers shrivelled, and I were gone?
What if the waters ceased, where were the marigolds then, and
    the gudgeon?
What is this thing that I look down upon?
White on the water wimples my shadow, strains like a dog on
    a string, to run on.

How it looks back, like a white dog to its master!
I on the bank all substance, my shadow all shadow looking up
   to me, looking back!
And the water runs, and runs faster, runs faster,
And the white dog dances and quivers, I am holding his cord
   quite slack.

But how splendid it is to be substance, here!
My shadow is neither here nor there; but I, I am royally here!
I am here! I am here! screams the peewit; the may-blobs burst
   out in a laugh as they hear!
Here! flick the rabbits. Here! pants the gorse. Here! say the
   insects far and near.

Over my skin in the sunshine, the warm, clinging air
Flushed with the songs of seven larks singing at once, goes
   kissing me glad.
You are here! You are here! We have found you! Everywhere
We sought you substantial, you touchstone of caresses, you
   naked lad!

Oh but the water loves me and folds me,
Plays with me, sways me, lifts me and sinks me, murmurs: Oh
   marvellous stuff!
No longer shadow! – and it holds me
Close, and it rolls me, enfolds me, touches me, as if never it
   could touch me enough.

Sun, but in substance, yellow water-blobs!
Wings and feathers on the crying, mysterious ages, peewits
   wheeling!
All that is right, all that is good, all that is God takes
   substance! a rabbit lobs
In confirmation, I hear sevenfold lark-songs pealing.

Dog-Tired

If she would come to me here
  Now the sunken swaths
  Are glittering paths
To the sun, and the swallows cut clear
Into the setting sun! if she came to me here!

If she would come to me now,
Before the last-mown harebells are dead;
While that vetch-clump still burns red!
Before all the bats have dropped from the bough
To cool in the night; if she came to me now!

The horses are untackled, the chattering machine
Is still at last. If she would come
We could gather up the dry hay from
The hill-brow, and lie quite still, till the green
Sky ceased to quiver, and lost its active sheen.

I should like to drop
On the hay, with my head on her knee,
And lie dead still, while she
Breathed quiet above me; and the crop
Of stars grew silently.

I should like to lie still
As if I was dead; but feeling
Her hand go stealing
Over my face and my head, until
This ache was shed.

The Collier's Wife

Somebody's knockin' at th' door
    Mother, come down an' see!
– I's think it's nobbut a beggar;
    Say I'm busy.

It's not a beggar, mother; hark
    How 'ard 'e knocks!
– Eh, tha'rt a mard-arsed kid,
    E'll gie thee socks!

Shout an' ax what 'e wants,
    I canna come down.
– 'E says, is it Arthur Holliday's?
    – Say Yes, tha clown.

'E says: Tell your mother as 'er mester's
    Got hurt i' th' pit –
What? Oh my Sirs, 'e never says that,
    That's not it!

Come out o' th' way an' let me see!
    Eh, there's no peace!
An' stop thy scraightin', childt,
    Do shut thy face!

'Your mester's 'ad a accident
    An' they ta'ein' 'im i' th' ambulance
Ter Nottingham.' – Eh dear o' me,
    If 'e's not a man for mischance!

Wheer's 'e hurt this time, lad?
    – I dunna know,
They on'y towd me it wor bad –
    It would be so!

Out o' my way, childt! dear o' me, wheer
   'Ave I put 'is clean stockin's an' shirt?
Goodness knows if they'll be able
   To take off 'is pit-dirt!

An' what a moan 'e'll make! there niver
   Was such a man for a fuss
If anything ailed 'im; at any rate
   I shan't 'ave 'im to nuss.

I do 'ope as it's not so very bad!
   Eh, what a shame it seems
As some should ha'e hardly a smite o' trouble
   An' others 'as reams!

It's a shame as 'e should be knocked about
   Like this, I'm sure it is!
'E's 'ad twenty accidents, if 'e's 'ad one;
   Owt bad, an' it's his!

There's one thing, we s'll 'ave a peaceful 'ouse f'r a bit,
   Thank heaven for a peaceful house!
An' there's compensation, sin' it's accident,
   An' club-money – I won't growse.

An' a fork an' a spoon 'e'll want – an' what else?
   I s'll never catch that train!
What a traipse it is, if a man gets hurt!
   I sh'd think 'e'll get right again.

Monologue of a Mother

This is the last of all, then, this is the last!
I must fold my hands, and turn my face to the fire,
And watch my dead days fusing together in dross,
Shape after shape, and scene after scene of my past
Clotting to one dead mass in the sinking fire
Where ash on the dying coals grows swiftly, like heavy moss.

Strange he is, my son, for whom I have waited like a lover;
Strange to me, like a captive in a foreign country, haunting
The confines, gazing out beyond, where the winds go free;
White and gaunt, with wistful eyes that hover
Always on the distance, as if his soul were chaunting
A monotonous weird of departure away from me.

Like a thin white bird blown out of the northern seas,
Like a bird from the far north blown with a broken wing
Into our sooty garden, he drags and beats
Along the fence perpetually, seeking release
From me, from the hand of my love which creeps up, needing
His happiness, whilst he in displeasure retreats.

I must look away from him, for my faded eyes
Like a cringing dog at his heels offend him now,
Like a toothless hound pursuing him with my will;
Till he chafes at my crouching persistence, and a sharp spark
    flies
In my soul from under the sudden frown of his brow
As he blenches and turns away, and my heart stands still.

This is the last, it will not be any more.
All my life I have borne the burden of myself,
All the long years of sitting in my husband's house;
Never have I said to myself as he closed the door;
'Now I am caught! You are hopelessly lost, O Self!
You are frightened with joy, my heart, like a frightened mouse.'

Three times have I offered myself, three times rejected.
It will not be any more. No more, my son, my son! –
Never to know the glad freedom of obedience, since long ago
The angel of childhood kissed me and went! I expected
This last one to claim me; – and now, my son, O my son,
I must sit alone and wait, and never know
The loss of myself, till death comes, who cannot fail.

Death, in whose service is nothing of gladness, takes me;
For the lips and the eyes of God are behind a veil.
And the thought of the lipless voice of the Father shakes me
With dread, and fills my heart with the tears of desire,
And my heart rebels with anguish, as night draws nigher.

The Best of School

The blinds are drawn because of the sun,
And the boys and the room in a colourless gloom
Of underwater float: bright ripples run
Across the walls as the blinds are blown
To let the sunlight in; and I,
As I sit on the shores of the class, alone,
Watch the boys in their summer blouses
As they write, their round heads busily bowed:
And one after another rouses
His face to look at me,
To ponder very quietly,
As seeing, he does not see.

And then he turns again, with a little, glad
Thrill of his work he turns again from me,
Having found what he wanted, having got what was to be
    had.

And very sweet it is, while the sunlight waves
In the ripening morning, to sit alone with the class
And feel the stream of awakening ripple and pass
From me to the boys, whose brightening souls it laves
For this little hour.

              This morning, sweet it is
To feel the lads' looks light on me,
Then back in a swift, bright flutter to work;
Each one darting away with his
Discovery, like birds that steal and flee.
Touch after touch I feel on me
As their eyes glance at me for the grain
Of rigour they taste delightedly.

As tendrils reach out yearningly,
Slowly rotate till they touch the tree

That they cleave unto, and up which they climb
Up to their lives – so they to me.

I feel them cling and cleave to me
As vines going eagerly up; they twine
My life with other leaves, my time
Is hidden in theirs, their thrills are mine.

Violets

Sister, tha knows while we was on th' planks
    Aside o' t' grave, an' th' coffin set
On th' yaller clay, wi' th' white flowers top of it
    Waitin' ter be buried out o' th' wet?

An' t' parson makin' haste, an' a' t' black
    Huddlin' up i' t' rain,
Did t' 'appen ter notice a bit of a lass way back
    Hoverin', lookin' poor an' plain?

    – How should I be lookin' round!
        An' me standin' there on th' plank,
    An' our Ted's coffin set on th' ground,
        Waitin' to be sank!

    I'd as much as I could do, to think
        Of 'im bein' gone
    That young, an' a' the fault of drink
        An' carryin's on! –

Let that be; 'appen it worna th' drink, neither,
Nor th' carryin' on as killed 'im.
                         – No, 'appen not,
My sirs! But I say 'twas! For a blither
Lad never stepped, till 'e got in with your lot. –

All right, all right, it's my fault! But let
Me tell about that lass. When you'd all gone
Ah stopped behind on t' pad, i' t' pourin' wet
An' watched what 'er 'ad on.

Tha should ha' seed 'er slive up when yer'd gone!
Tha should ha' seed 'er kneel an' look in
At th' sloppy grave! an' 'er little neck shone
That white, an' 'er cried that much, I'd like to begin

Scraightin' mysen as well. 'Er undid 'er black
Jacket at th' bosom, an' took out
Over a double 'andful o' violets, a' in a pack
An' white an' blue in a ravel, like a clout.

An' warm, for th' smell come waftin' to me. 'Er put 'er face
Right in 'em, an' scraighted a bit again,
Then after a bit 'er dropped 'em down that place,
An' I come away, acause o' th' teemin' rain.

But I thowt ter mysen, as that wor th' only bit
O' warmth as 'e got down theer; th' rest wor stone cold.
From that bit of a wench's bosom; 'e'd be glad of it,
Gladder nor of thy lilies, if tha maun be told.

End of Another Home Holiday

When shall I see the half-moon sink again
Behind the black sycamore at the end of the garden?
When will the scent of the dim white phlox
Creep up the wall to me, and in at my open window?

Why is it, the long, slow stroke of the midnight bell
　　　(Will it never finish the twelve?)
Falls again and again on my heart with a heavy reproach?

The moon-mist is over the village, out of the mist speaks the
　　bell,
And all the little roofs of the village bow low, pitiful,
　　beseeching, resigned.
– Speak, you my home! what is it I don't do well?

Ah home, suddenly I love you
As I hear the sharp clean trot of a pony down the road,
Succeeding sharp little sounds dropping into silence
Clear upon the long-drawn hoarseness of a train across the
　　valley.
　　　　　　· · · · · ·
The light has gone out, from under my mother's door.
　　　That she should love me so! –
　　　She, so lonely, greying now!
　　　And I leaving her,
　　　Bent on my pursuits!

　　　　Love is the great Asker.
　　　　The sun and the rain do not ask the secret
　　　　Of the time when the grain struggles down in the dark.
　　　　The moon walks her lonely way without anguish,
　　　　Because no-one grieves over her departure.

Forever, ever by my shoulder pitiful love will linger,
Crouching as little houses crouch under the mist when I turn.

14

Forever, out of the mist, the church lifts up a reproachful
  finger,
Pointing my eyes in wretched defiance where love hides her
  face to mourn.

> Oh! but the rain creeps down to wet the grain
> That struggles alone in the dark,
> And asking nothing, patiently steals back again!
> The moon sets forth o' nights
> To walk the lonely, dusky heights
> Serenely, with steps unswerving;
> Pursued by no sigh of bereavement,
> No tears of love unnerving
> Her constant tread:
> While ever at my side,
> Frail and sad, with grey, bowed head,
> The beggar-woman, the yearning-eyed
> Inexorable love goes lagging.

The wild young heifer, glancing distraught,
With a strange new knocking of life at her side
  Runs seeking a loneliness.
The little grain draws down the earth, to hide.
Nay, even the slumberous egg, as it labours under the shell
  Patiently to divide and self-divide,
Asks to be hidden, and wishes nothing to tell.

But when I draw the scanty cloak of silence over my eyes
Piteous love comes peering under the hood;
Touches the clasp with trembling fingers, and tries
To put her ear to the painful sob of my blood;
While her tears soak through to my breast,
> Where they burn and cauterise.

> · · · · · ·

> The moon lies back and reddens.
> In the valley a corncrake calls
>   Monotonously,

15

With a plaintive, unalterable voice, that deadens
    My confident activity;
With a hoarse, insistent request that falls
    Unweariedly, unweariedly,
    Asking something more of me,
        Yet more of me.

Baby Running Barefoot

When the white feet of the baby beat across the grass
The little white feet nod like white flowers in a wind,
They poise and run like puffs of wind that pass
Over water where the weeds are thinned.

And the sight of their white playing in the grass
Is winsome as a robin's song, so fluttering;
Or like two butterflies that settle on a glass
Cup for a moment, soft little wing-beats uttering.

And I wish that the baby would tack across here to me
Like a wind-shadow running on a pond, so she could stand
With two little bare white feet upon my knee
And I could feel her feet in either hand

Cool as syringa buds in morning hours,
Or firm and silken as young peony flowers.

Guards

Where the trees rise like cliffs, proud and blue-tinted in the
    distance,
Between the cliffs of the trees, on the grey-green park
Rests a still line of soldiers, red, motionless range of guards
Smouldering with darkened busbies beneath the bayonets'
    slant rain.

Colossal in nearness a blue police sits still on his horse
Guarding the path; his hand relaxed at his thigh,
And skywards his face is immobile, eyelids aslant
In tedium, and mouth relaxed as if smiling – ineffable tedium!

So! So! Gaily a general canters across the space,
With white plumes blinking under the evening grey sky.
And suddenly, as if the ground moved,
The red range heaves in slow, magnetic reply.

EVOLUTIONS OF SOLDIERS

The red range heaves and compulsory sways, ah see! in the
    flush of a march.
Softly-impulsive advancing as water towards a weir from the
    arch
Of shadow emerging as blood emerges from inward shades of
    our night
Encroaching towards a crisis, a meeting, a spasm and throb of
    delight.

The wave of soldiers, the coming wave, the throbbing red
    breast of approach
Upon us; dark eyes as here beneath the busbies glittering, dark
    threats that broach

Our beached vessel; darkened rencontre inhuman, and closed
    warm lips, and dark
Mouth-hair of soldiers passing above us, over the wreck of
    our bark.

And so, it is ebb-time, they turn, the eyes beneath the busbies
    are gone.
But the blood has suspended its timbre, the heart from out of
    oblivion
Knows but the retreat of the burning shoulders, the red-swift
    waves of the sweet
Fire horizontal declining and ebbing, the twilit ebb of retreat.

Aware

Slowly the moon is rising out of the ruddy haze,
Divesting herself of her golden shift, and so
Emerging white and exquisite; and I in amaze
See in the sky before me, a woman I did not know
I loved, but there she goes, and her beauty hurts my heart;
I follow her down the night, begging her not to depart.

A Pang of Reminiscence

High and smaller goes the moon, she is small and very far
    from me,
Wistful and candid, watching me wistfully from her distance,
    and I see
Trembling blue in her pallor a tear that surely I have seen
    before,
A tear which I had hoped that even hell held not again in
    store.

Sorrow

Why does the thin grey strand
Floating up from the forgotten
Cigarette between my fingers,
Why does it trouble me?

Ah, you will understand;
When I carried my mother downstairs,
A few times only, at the beginning
Of her soft-foot malady,

I should find, for a reprimand
To my gaiety, a few long grey hairs
On the breast of my coat; and one by one
I watched them float up the dark chimney.

Piano

Softly, in the dusk, a woman is singing to me;
Taking me back down the vista of years, till I see
A child sitting under the piano, in the boom of the tingling
    strings
And pressing the small, poised feet of a mother who smiles as
    she sings.

In spite of myself, the insidious mastery of song
Betrays me back, till the heart of me weeps to belong
To the old Sunday evenings at home, with winter outside
And hymns in the cosy parlour, the tinkling piano our guide.

So now it is vain for the singer to burst into clamour
With the great black piano appassionato. The glamour
Of childish days is upon me, my manhood is cast
Down in the flood of remembrance, I weep like a child for the
    past.

Disagreeable Advice

Always, sweetheart,
Carry into your room the blossoming boughs of cherry,
Almond and apple and pear diffuse with light, that very
Soon strews itself on the floor; and keep the radiance of
   spring
Fresh quivering; keep the sunny-swift March-days waiting
In a little throng at your door, and admit the one who is
   plaiting
Her hair for womanhood, and play awhile with her, then bid
   her depart.

A come and go of March-day loves
Through the flower-vine, trailing screen;
   A fluttering in of doves.
Then a launch abroad of shrinking doves
Over the waste where no hope is seen
Of open hands:
           Dance in and out
Small-bosomed girls of the spring of love,
With a bubble of laughter, and shrilly shout
Of mirth; then the dripping of tears on your glove.

Restlessness

At the open door of the room I stand and look at the night,
Hold my hand to catch the raindrops, that slant into sight,
Arriving grey from the darkness above suddenly into the light
    of the room.
I will escape from the hollow room, the box of light,
And be out in the bewildering darkness, which is always
    fecund, which might
Mate my hungry soul with a germ of its womb.

I will go out to the night, as a man goes down to the shore
To draw his net through the surf's thin line, at the dawn
    before
The sun warms the sea, little, lonely and sad, sifting the
    sobbing tide.
I will sift the surf that edges the night, with my net, the four
Strands of my eyes and my lips and my hands and my feet,
    sifting the store
Of flotsam until my soul is tired or satisfied.

I will catch in my eyes' quick net
The faces of all the women as they go past,
Bend over them with my soul, to cherish the wet
Cheeks and wet hair a moment, saying: 'Is it you?'
Looking earnestly under the dark umbrellas, held fast
Against the wind; and if, where the lamplight blew
Its rainy swill about us, she answered me
With a laugh and a merry wildness that it was she
Who was seeking me, and had found me at last to free
Me now from the stunting bonds of my chastity,
How glad I should be!

Moving along in the mysterious ebb of the night
Pass the men whose eyes are shut like anemones in a dark
    pool;

Why don't they open with vision and speak to me? what have
    they in sight?
Why do I wander aimless among them, desirous fool?

I can always linger over the huddled books on the stalls,
Always gladden my amorous fingers with the touch of their
    leaves,
Always kneel in courtship to the shelves in the doorways,
    where falls
The shadow, always offer myself to one mistress, who always
    receives.

But oh, it is not enough, it is all no good.
There is something I want to feel in my running blood,
Something I want to touch; I must hold my face to the rain,
I must hold my face to the wind, and let it explain
Me its life as it hurries in secret.
I will trail my hands again through the drenched, cold leaves
Till my hands are full of the chillness and touch of leaves,
Till at length they induce me to sleep, and to forget.

Moonrise

And who has seen the moon, who has not seen
Her rise from out the chamber of the deep,
Flushed and grand and naked, as from the chamber
Of finished bridegroom, seen her rise and throw
Confession of delight upon the wave,
Littering the waves with her own superscription
Of bliss, till all her lambent beauty shakes towards us
Spread out and known at last, and we are sure
That beauty is a thing beyond the grave,
That perfect, bright experience never falls
To nothingness, and time will dim the moon
Sooner than our full consummation here
In this odd life will tarnish or pass away.

Mutilation

A thick mist-sheet lies over the broken wheat.
I walk up to my neck in mist, holding my mouth up.
Across there, a discoloured moon burns itself out.

I hold the night in horror;
I dare not turn round.

To-night I have left her alone.
They would have it I have left her for ever.

Oh my God, how it aches
Where she is cut off from me!

Perhaps she will go back to England.
Perhaps she will go back,
Perhaps we are parted for ever.

If I go on walking through the whole breadth of Germany
I come to the North Sea, or the Baltic.

Over there is Russia – Austria, Switzerland, France, in a circle!
I here in the undermist on the Bavarian road.

It aches in me.
What is England or France, far off,
But a name she might take?
I don't mind this continent stretching, the sea far away;
It aches in me for her
Like the agony of limbs cut off and aching;
Not even longing,
It is only agony.

A cripple!
Oh God, to be mutilated!
To be a cripple!

And if I never see her again?

I think, if they told me so
I could convulse the heavens with my horror.
I think I could alter the frame of things in my agony.
I think I could break the System with my heart.
I think, in my convulsion, the skies would break.

She too suffers.
But who could compel her, if she chose me against them all?
She has not chosen me finally, she suspends her choice.
Night folk, Tuatha De Danaan, dark Gods, govern her sleep,
Magnificent ghosts of the darkness, carry off her decision in
    sleep,
Leave her no choice, make her lapse me-ward, make her,
Oh Gods of the living Darkness, powers of Night.

  Wolfratshausen

Green

The dawn was apple-green,
  The sky was green wine held up in the sun,
The moon was a golden petal between.

She opened her eyes, and green
  They shone, clear like flowers undone
For the first time, now for the first time seen.

  Icking

River Roses

By the Isar, in the twilight
We were wandering and singing,
By the Isar, in the evening
We climbed the huntsman's ladder and sat swinging
In the fir-tree overlooking the marshes,
While river met with river, and the ringing
Of their pale-green glacier water filled the evening.

By the Isar, in the twilight
We found the dark wild roses
Hanging red at the river; and simmering
Frogs were singing, and over the river closes
Was savour of ice and of roses; and glimmering
Fear was abroad. We whispered: 'No one knows us.
Let it be as the snake disposes
Here in this simmering marsh.'

Kloster Schaeftlarn

Gloire de Dijon

When she rises in the morning
I linger to watch her;
She spreads the bath-cloth underneath the window
And the sunbeams catch her
Glistening white on the shoulders,
While down her sides the mellow
Golden shadow glows as
She stoops to the sponge, and her swung breasts
Sway like full-blown yellow
Gloire de Dijon roses.

She drips herself with water, and her shoulders
Glisten as silver, they crumple up
Like wet and falling roses, and I listen
For the sluicing of their rain-dishevelled petals.
In the window full of sunlight
Concentrates her golden shadow
Fold on fold, until it glows as
Mellow as the glory roses.

   Icking

Song of a Man Who Has Come Through

Not I, not I, but the wind that blows through me!
A fine wind is blowing the new direction of Time.
If only I let it bear me, carry me, if only it carry me!
If only I am sensitive, subtle, oh, delicate, a winged gift!
If only, most lovely of all, I yield myself and am borrowed
By the fine, fine wind that takes its course through the chaos
   of the world
Like a fine, an exquisite chisel, a wedge-blade inserted;
If only I am keen and hard like the sheer tip of a wedge
Driven by invisible blows,
The rock will split, we shall come at the wonder, we shall find
   the Hesperides.

Oh, for the wonder that bubbles into my soul,
I would be a good fountain, a good well-head,
Would blur no whisper, spoil no expression.

What is the knocking?
What is the knocking at the door in the night?
It is somebody wants to do us harm.

No, no, it is the three strange angels.
Admit them, admit them.

Pomegranate

You tell me I am wrong.
Who are you, who is anybody to tell me I am wrong?
I am not wrong.

In Syracuse, rock left bare by the viciousness of Greek
    women,
No doubt you have forgotten the pomegranate-trees in
    flower,
Oh so red, and such a lot of them.

Whereas at Venice,
Abhorrent, green, slippery city
Whose Doges were old, and had ancient eyes,
In the dense foliage of the inner garden
Pomegranates like bright green stone,
And barbed, barbed with a crown.
Oh, crown of spiked green metal
Actually growing!

Now in Tuscany,
Pomegranates to warm your hands at;
And crowns, kingly, generous, tilting crowns
Over the left eyebrow.

And, if you dare, the fissure!

Do you mean to tell me you will see no fissure?
Do you prefer to look on the plain side?

For all that, the setting suns are open.
The end cracks open with the beginning:
Rosy, tender, glittering within the fissure.

Do you mean to tell me there should be no fissure?
No glittering, compact drops of dawn?

Do you mean it is wrong, the gold-filmed skin, integument,
  shown ruptured?

For my part, I prefer my heart to be broken.
It is so lovely, dawn-kaleidoscopic within the crack.

  San Gervasio in Tuscany

Peach

Would you like to throw a stone at me?
Here, take all that's left of my peach.

Blood-red, deep;
Heaven knows how it came to pass.
Somebody's pound of flesh rendered up.

Wrinkled with secrets
And hard with the intention to keep them.

Why, from silvery peach-bloom,
From that shallow-silvery wine-glass on a short stem
This rolling, dropping, heavy globule?

I am thinking, of course, of the peach before I ate it.

Why so velvety, why so voluptuous heavy?
Why hanging with such inordinate weight?
Why so indented?

Why the groove?
Why the lovely, bivalve roundnesses?
Why the ripple down the sphere?
Why the suggestion of incision?

Why was not my peach round and finished like a billiard ball?
It would have been if man had made it.
Though I've eaten it now.

But it wasn't round and finished like a billiard ball.
And because I say so, you would like to throw something at
    me.

Here, you can have my peach stone.

San Gervasio

36

Medlars and Sorb-Apples

I love you, rotten,
Delicious rottenness.

I love to suck you out from your skins
So brown and soft and coming suave,
So morbid, as the Italians say.

What a rare, powerful, reminiscent flavour
Comes out of your falling through the stages of decay:
Stream within stream.

Something of the same flavour as Syracusan muscat wine
Or vulgar Marsala.

Though even the word Marsala will smack of preciosity
Soon in the pussyfoot West.

What is it?
What is it, in the grape turning raisin,
In the medlar, in the sorb-apple,
Wineskins of brown morbidity,
Autumnal excrementa;
What is it that reminds us of white gods?

Gods nude as blanched nut-kernels,
Strangely, half-sinisterly flesh-fragrant
As if with sweat,
And drenched with mystery.

Sorb-apples, medlars with dead crowns.
I say, wonderful are the hellish experiences,
Orphic, delicate
Dionysos of the Underworld.

A kiss, and a spasm of farewell, a moment's orgasm of
    rupture,
Then along the damp road alone, till the next turning.

37

And there, a new partner, a new parting, a new unfusing into
   twain,
A new gasp of further isolation,
A new intoxication of loneliness, among decaying, frost-cold
   leaves.

Going down the strange lanes of hell, more and more
   intensely alone,
The fibres of the heart parting one after the other
And yet the soul continuing, naked-footed, ever more vividly
   embodied
Like a flame blown whiter and whiter
In a deeper and deeper darkness
Ever more exquisite, distilled in separation.

So, in the strange retorts of medlars and sorb-apples
The distilled essence of hell.
The exquisite odour of leave-taking.
         Jamque vale!
Orpheus, and the winding, leaf-clogged, silent lanes of hell.

Each soul departing with its own isolation,
Strangest of all strange companions,
And best.

Medlars, sorb-apples,
More than sweet
Flux of autumn
Sucked out of your empty bladders

And sipped down, perhaps, with a sip of Marsala
So that the rambling, sky-dropped grape can add its savour to
   yours,
Orphic farewell, and farewell, and farewell
And the *ego sum* of Dionysos
The *sono io* of perfect drunkenness
Intoxication of final loneliness.

   San Gervasio

38

Figs

The proper way to eat a fig, in society,
Is to split it in four, holding it by the stump,
And open it, so that it is a glittering, rosy, moist, honied,
   heavy-petalled four-petalled flower.

Then you throw away the skin
Which is just like a four-sepalled calyx,
After you have taken off the blossom with your lips.

But the vulgar way
Is just to put your mouth to the crack, and take out the flesh
   in one bite.

Every fruit has its secret.

The fig is a very secretive fruit.
As you see it standing growing, you feel at once it is symbolic:
And it seems male.
But when you come to know it better, you agree with the
   Romans, it is female.

The Italians vulgarly say, it stands for the female part; the
   fig-fruit:
The fissure, the yoni,
The wonderful moist conductivity towards the centre.

Involved,
Inturned,
The flowering all inward and womb-fibrilled;
And but one orifice.

The fig, the horse-shoe, the squash-blossom.
Symbols.

There was a flower that flowered inward, womb-ward;
Now there is a fruit like a ripe womb.

It was always a secret.
That's how it should be, the female should always be secret.
There never was any standing aloft and unfolded on a
    bough
Like other flowers, in a revelation of petals;
Silver-pink peach, venetian green glass of medlars and
    sorb-apples,
Shallow wine-cups on short, bulging stems
Openly pledging heaven:
Here's to the thorn in flower! Here is to Utterance!
The brave, adventurous rosaceæ.

Folded upon itself, and secret unutterable,
And milky-sapped, sap that curdles milk and makes *ricotta*,
Sap that smells strange on your fingers, that even goats won't
    taste it;
Folded upon itself, enclosed like any Mohammedan woman,
Its nakedness all within-walls, its flowering forever unseen,
One small way of access only, and this close-curtained from
    the light;
Fig, fruit of the female mystery, covert and inward,
Mediterranean fruit, with your covert nakedness,
Where everything happens invisible, flowering and
    fertilisation, and fruiting
In the inwardness of your you, that eye will never see
Till it's finished, and you're over-ripe, and you burst to give up
    your ghost.

Till the drop of ripeness exudes,
And the year is over.

And then the fig has kept her secret long enough.
So it explodes, and you see through the fissure the scarlet.
And the fig is finished, the year is over.

That's how the fig dies, showing her crimson through the
    purple slit
Like a wound, the exposure of her secret, on the open day.

Like a prostitute, the bursten fig, making a show of her
    secret.

That's how women die too.

The year is fallen over-ripe,
The year of our women.
The year of our women is fallen over-ripe.
The secret is laid bare.
And rottenness soon sets in.
The year of our women is fallen over-ripe.

When Eve once knew *in her mind* that she was naked
She quickly sewed fig-leaves, and sewed the same for the
    man.
She'd been naked all her days before,
But till then, till that apple of knowledge, she hadn't had the
    fact on her mind.

She got the fact on her mind, and quickly sewed fig-leaves.
And women have been sewing ever since.
But now they stitch to adorn the bursten fig, not to cover it.
They have their nakedness more than ever on their mind,
And they won't let us forget it.

Now, the secret
Becomes an affirmation through moist, scarlet lips
That laugh at the Lord's indignation.

What then, good Lord! cry the women.
We have kept our secret long enough.
We are a ripe fig.
Let us burst into affirmation.

They forget, ripe figs won't keep.
Ripe figs won't keep.

Honey-white figs of the north, black figs with scarlet inside, of
    the south.
Ripe figs won't keep, won't keep in any clime.

What then, when women the world over have all bursten into
    self-assertion?
And bursten figs won't keep?

San Gervasio

Cypresses

Tuscan cypresses,
What is it?

Folded in like a dark thought
For which the language is lost,
Tuscan cypresses,
Is there a great secret?
Are our words no good?

The undeliverable secret,
Dead with a dead race and a dead speech, and yet
Darkly monumental in you,
Etruscan cypresses.

Ah, how I admire your fidelity,
Dark cypresses!

Is it the secret of the long-nosed Etruscans?
The long-nosed, sensitive-footed, subtly-smiling Etruscans,
Who made so little noise outside the cypress groves?

Among the sinuous, flame-tall cypresses
That swayed their length of darkness all around
Etruscan-dusky, wavering men of old Etruria:
Naked except for fanciful long shoes,
Going with insidious, half-smiling quietness
And some of Africa's imperturbable sang-froid
About a forgotten business.

What business, then?
Nay, tongues are dead, and words are hollow as hollow
    seed-pods,
Having shed their sound and finished all their echoing
Etruscan syllables,
That had the telling.

Yet more I see you darkly concentrate,
Tuscan cypresses,
On one old thought:
On one old slim imperishable thought, while you remain
Etruscan cypresses;
Dusky, slim marrow-thought of slender, flickering men of
    Etruria,
Whom Rome called vicious.

Vicious, dark cypresses:
Vicious, you supple, brooding, softly-swaying pillars of dark
    flame.
Monumental to a dead, dead race
Embowered in you!

Were they then vicious, the slender, tender-footed
Long-nosed men of Etruria?
Or was their way only evasive and different, dark, like
    cypress-trees in a wind?

They are dead, with all their vices,
And all that is left
Is the shadowy monomania of some cypresses
And tombs.

The smile, the subtle Etruscan smile still lurking
Within the tombs,
Etruscan cypresses.
He laughs longest who laughs last;
Nay, Leonardo only bungled the pure Etruscan smile.

What would I not give
To bring back the rare and orchid-like
Evil-yclept Etruscan?
For as to the evil
We have only Roman word for it,
Which I, being a little weary of Roman virtue,
Don't hang much weight on.

For oh, I know, in the dust where we have buried
The silenced races and all their abominations,
We have buried so much of the delicate magic of life.

There in the deeps
That churn the frankincense and ooze the myrrh,
Cypress shadowy,
Such an aroma of lost human life!

They say the fit survive,
But I invoke the spirits of the lost.
Those that have not survived, the darkly lost, ·
To bring their meaning back into life again,
Which they have taken away
And wrapt inviolable in soft cypress-trees,
Etruscan cypresses.

Evil, what is evil?
There is only one evil, to deny life
As Rome denied Etruria
And mechanical America Montezuma still.

    Fiesole

Bare Fig-Trees

Fig-trees, weird fig-trees
Made of thick smooth silver,
Made of sweet, untarnished silver in the sea-southern air —
I say untarnished, but I mean opaque —
Thick, smooth-fleshed silver, dull only as human limbs are dull
With the life-lustre,
Nude with the dim light of full, healthy life
That is always half-dark,
And suave like passion-flower petals,
Like passion-flowers,
With the half-secret gleam of a passion-flower hanging from
    the rock,
Great, complicated, nude fig-tree, stemless flower-mesh,
Flowerily naked in flesh, and giving off hues of life.

Rather like an octopus, but strange and sweet-myriad-limbed
    octopus;
Like a nude, like a rock-living, sweet-fleshed sea-anemone,
Flourishing from the rock in a mysterious arrogance.

Let me sit down beneath the many-branching candelabrum
That lives upon this rock
And laugh at Time, and laugh at dull Eternity,
And make a joke of stale Infinity,
Within the flesh-scent of this wicked tree,
That has kept so many secrets up its sleeve,
And has been laughing through so many ages
At man and his uncomfortablenesses,
And his attempt to assure himself that what is so is not so,
Up its sleeve.

Let me sit down beneath this many-branching candelabrum,
The Jewish seven-branched, tallow-stinking candlestick kicked
    over the cliff

And all its tallow righteousness got rid of,
And let me notice it behave itself.

And watch it putting forth each time to heaven,
Each time straight to heaven,
With marvellous naked assurance each single twig,
Each one setting off straight to the sky
As if it were the leader, the main-stem, the forerunner,
Intent to hold the candle of the sun upon its socket-tip,
It alone.

Every young twig
No sooner issued sideways from the thigh of his predecessor
Than off he starts without a qualm
To hold the one and only lighted candle of the sun in his
    socket-tip.
He casually gives birth to another young bud from his thigh,
Which at once sets off to be the one and only,
And hold the lighted candle of the sun.

Oh many-branching candelabrum, oh strange up-starting
    fig-tree,
Oh weird Demos, where every twig is the arch twig,
Each imperiously over-equal to each, equality over-reaching
    itself
Like the snakes on Medusa's head,
Oh naked fig-tree!

Still, no doubt every one of you can be the sun-socket as well
    as every other of you.
Demos, Demos, Demos!
Demon, too,
Wicked fig-tree, equality puzzle, with your self-conscious
    secret fruits.

Taormina

47

Bare Almond-Trees

Wet almond-trees, in the rain,
Like iron sticking grimly out of earth;
Black almond trunks, in the rain,
Like iron implements twisted, hideous, out of the earth,
Out of the deep, soft fledge of Sicilian winter-green,
Earth-grass uneatable,
Almond trunks curving blackly, iron-dark, climbing the slopes.

Almond-tree, beneath the terrace rail,
Black, rusted, iron trunk,
You have welded your thin stems finer,
Like steel, like sensitive steel in the air,
Grey, lavender, sensitive steel, curving thinly and brittly up in
    a parabola.

What are you doing in the December rain?
Have you a strange electric sensitiveness in your steel tips?
Do you feel the air for electric influences
Like some strange magnetic apparatus?
Do you take in messages, in some strange code,
From heaven's wolfish, wandering electricity, that prowls so
    constantly round Etna?
Do you take the whisper of sulphur from the air?
Do you hear the chemical accents of the sun?
Do you telephone the roar of the waters over the earth?
And from all this, do you make calculations?

Sicily, December's Sicily in a mass of rain
With iron branching blackly, rusted like old, twisted
    implements
And brandishing and stooping over earth's wintry fledge,
    climbing the slopes
Of uneatable soft green!

Taormina

48

Southern Night

Come up, thou red thing.
Come up, and be called a moon.

The mosquitoes are biting to-night
Like memories.

Memories, northern memories,
Bitter-stinging white world that bore us
Subsiding into this night.

Call it moonrise
This red anathema?

Rise, thou red thing,
Unfold slowly upwards, blood-dark;
Burst the night's membrane of tranquil stars
Finally.

Maculate
The red Macula.

Taormina

Almond Blossom

Even iron can put forth,
Even iron.

This is the iron age,
But let us take heart
Seeing iron break and bud,
Seeing rusty iron puff with clouds of blossom.

The almond-tree,
December's bare iron hooks sticking out of earth.

The almond-tree,
That knows the deadliest poison, like a snake
In supreme bitterness.

Upon the iron, and upon the steel,
Odd flakes as if of snow, odd bits of snow,
Odd crumbs of melting snow.

But you mistake, it is not from the sky;
From out the iron, and from out the steel,
Flying not down from heaven, but storming up,
Strange storming up from the dense under-earth
Along the iron, to the living steel
In rose-hot tips, and flakes of rose-pale snow
Setting supreme annunciation to the world.

Nay, what a heart of delicate super-faith,
Iron-breaking.
The rusty swords of almond-trees.

Trees suffer, like races, down the long ages.
They wander and are exiled, they live in exile through long
    ages
Like drawn blades never sheathed, hacked and gone black,
The alien trees in alien lands: and yet

The heart of blossom,
The unquenchable heart of blossom!

Look at the many-cicatrised frail vine, none more scarred and
    frail,
Yet see him fling himself abroad in fresh abandon
From the small wound-stump.

Even the wilful, obstinate, gummy fig-tree
Can be kept down, but he'll burst like a polyp into prolixity.

And the almond-tree, in exile, in the iron age!

This is the ancient southern earth whence the vases were
    baked, amphoras, craters, cantharus, œnochœ, and
    open-hearted cylix,
Bristling now with the iron of almond-trees

Iron, but unforgotten.
Iron, dawn-hearted,
Ever-beating dawn-heart, enveloped in iron against the exile,
    against the ages.

See it come forth in blossom
From the snow-remembering heart
In long-nighted January,
In the long dark nights of the evening star, and Sirius, and the
    Etna snow-wind through the long night.

Sweating his drops of blood through the long-nighted
    Gethsemane
Into blossom, into pride, into honey-triumph, into most
    exquisite splendour.
Oh, give me the tree of life in blossom
And the Cross sprouting its superb and fearless flowers!

Something must be reassuring to the almond, in the evening
    star, and the snow-wind, and the long, long nights,
Some memory of far, sun-gentler lands,
So that the faith in his heart smiles again

And his blood ripples with that untellable delight of
    once-more-vindicated faith,
And the Gethsemane blood at the iron pores unfolds, unfolds,
Pearls itself into tenderness of bud
And in a great and sacred forthcoming steps forth, steps out
    in one stride
A naked tree of blossom, like a bridegroom bathing in dew,
    divested of cover,
Frail-naked, utterly uncovered
To the green night-baying of the dog-star, Etna's snow-edged
    wind
And January's loud-seeming sun.
Think of it, from the iron fastness
Suddenly to dare to come out naked, in perfection of
    blossom, beyond the sword-rust.
Think, to stand there in full-unfolded nudity, smiling,
With all the snow-wind, and the sun-glare, and the dog-star
    baying epithalamion.

Oh, honey-bodied beautiful one,
Come forth from iron,
Red your heart is.
Fragile-tender, fragile-tender life-body,
More fearless than iron all the time,
And so much prouder, so disdainful of reluctances.

In the distance like boar-frost, like silvery ghosts communing
    on a green hill,
Hoar-frost-like and mysterious.

In the garden raying out
With a body like spray, dawn-tender, and looking about
With such insuperable, subtly-smiling assurance,
Sword-blade-born.

Unpromised,
No bounds being set.

Flaked out and come unpromised,
The tree being life-divine,
Fearing nothing, life-blissful at the core
Within iron and earth.
Knots of pink, fish-silvery
In heaven, in blue, blue heaven,
Soundless, bliss-full, wide rayed, honey-bodied,
Red at the core,
Red at the core,
Knotted in heaven upon the fine light.

Open,
Open,
Five times wide open,
Six times wide open,
And given, and perfect;
And red at the core with the last sore-heartedness,
Sore-hearted-looking.

   Fontana Vecchia

Sicilian Cyclamens

When he pushed his bush of black hair off his brow:
When she lifted her mop from her eyes, and screwed it in a
    knob behind
        – O act of fearful temerity!
When they felt their foreheads bare, naked to heaven, their
    eyes revealed:
When they felt the light of heaven brandished like a knife at
    their defenceless eyes,
And the sea like a blade at their face,
Mediterranean savages:
When they came out, face-revealed, under heaven, from the
    shaggy undergrowth of their own hair
For the first time,
They saw tiny rose cyclamens between their toes, growing
Where the slow toads sat brooding on the past.

Slow toads, and cyclamen leaves
Stickily glistening with eternal shadow
Keeping to earth.
Cyclamen leaves
Toad-filmy, earth-iridescent
Beautiful
Frost-filigreed
Spumed with mud
Snail-nacreous
Low down.

The shaking aspect of the sea
And man's defenceless bare face
And cyclamens putting their ears back.
Long, pensive, slim-muzzled greyhound buds
Dreamy, not yet present,
Drawn out of earth
At his toes.

Dawn-rose
Sub-delighted, stone-engendered
Cyclamens, young cyclamens
Arching
Waking, pricking their ears
Like delicate very-young greyhound bitches
Half-yawning at the open, inexperienced
Vista of day,
Folding back their soundless petalled ears.

Greyhound bitches
Bending their rosy muzzles pensive down,
And breathing soft, unwilling to wake to the new day
Yet sub-delighted.

Ah Mediterranean morning, when our world began!
Far-off Mediterranean mornings,
Pelasgic faces uncovered,
And unbudding cyclamens.

The hare suddenly goes uphill
Laying back her long ears with unwinking bliss.

And up the pallid, sea-blenched Mediterranean stone-slopes
Rose cyclamen, ecstatic fore-runner!
Cyclamens, ruddy-muzzled cyclamens
In little bunches like bunches of wild hares
Muzzles together, ears-aprick,
Whispering witchcraft
Like women at a well, the dawn-fountain.

Greece, and the world's morning
Where all the Parthenon marbles still fostered the roots of the
    cyclamen.
Violets
Pagan, rosy-muzzled violets
Autumnal
Dawn-pink,

Dawn-pale
Among squat toad-leaves sprinkling the unborn
Erechtheion marbles.

   Taormina

Hibiscus and Salvia Flowers

Hark! Hark!
The dogs do bark!
It's the socialists come to town,
None in rags and none in tags,
Swaggering up and down.

Sunday morning,
And from the Sicilian townlets skirting Etna
The socialists have gathered upon us, to look at us.

How shall we know them when we see them?
How shall we know them now they've come?

Not by their rags and not by their tags,
Nor by any distinctive gown;
The same unremarkable Sunday suit
And hats cocked up and down.

Yet there they are, youths, loutishly
Strolling in gangs and staring along the Corso
With the gang-stare
And a half-threatening envy
At every *forestière*,
Every lordly tuppenny foreigner from the hotels, fattening on
    the exchange.

Hark! Hark!
The dogs do bark!
It's the socialists in the town.
Sans rags, sans tags,
Sans beards, sans bags,
Sans any distinction at all except loutish commonness.

How do we know then, that they are they?
Bolshevists.
Leninists.

Communists.
Socialists.
-Ists! -Ists!

Alas, salvia and hibiscus flowers.
Salvia and hibiscus flowers.

Listen again.
Salvia and hibiscus flowers.
Is it not so?
Salvia and hibiscus flowers.

Hark! Hark!
The dogs do bark!
Salvia and hibiscus flowers.

Who smeared their doors with blood?
Who on their breasts
Put salvias and hibiscus?

Rosy, rosy scarlet,
And flame-rage, golden-throated
Bloom along the Corso on the living, perambulating bush.

Who said they might assume these blossoms?
What god did they consult?

Rose-red, princess hibiscus, rolling her pointed Chinese
    petals!
Azalea and camellia, single peony
And pomegranate bloom and scarlet mallow-flower
And all the eastern, exquisite royal plants
That noble blood has brought us down the ages!
Gently nurtured, frail and splendid
Hibiscus flower –
Alas, the Sunday coats of Sicilian bolshevists!

Pure blood, and noble blood, in the fine and rose-red veins;
Small, interspersed with jewels of white gold
Frail-filigreed among the rest;

Rose of the oldest races of princesses, Polynesian
Hibiscus.

Eve, in her happy moments,
Put hibiscus in her hair,
Before she humbled herself, and knocked her knees with
    repentance.

Sicilian bolshevists,
With hibiscus flowers in the buttonholes of your Sunday suits,
Come now, speaking of rights, what right have you to this
    flower?

The exquisite and ageless aristocracy
Of a peerless soul,
Blessed are the pure in heart and the fathomless in bright
    pride;
The loveliness that knows *noblesse oblige*;
The native royalty of red hibiscus flowers;
The exquisite assertion of new delicate life
Risen from the roots:
Is this how you'll have it, red-decked socialists,
Hibiscus-breasted?

If it be so, I fly to join you,
And if it be not so, brutes to pull down hibiscus flowers!

Or salvia!
Or dragon-mouthed salvia with gold throat of wrath!
Flame-flushed, enraged, splendid salvia,
Cock-crested, crowing your orange scarlet like a tocsin
Along the Corso all this Sunday morning.

Is your wrath red as salvias,
You socialists?
You with your grudging, envious, furtive rage,
In Sunday suits and yellow boots along the Corso.
You look well with your salvia flowers, I must say.

Warrior-like, dawn-cock's-comb flaring flower
Shouting forth flame to set the world on fire,
The dust-heap of man's filthy world on fire,
And burn it down, the glutted, stuffy world,
And feed the young new fields of life with ash,
With ash I say,
Bolshevists,
Your ashes even, my friends,
Among much other ash.

If there were salvia-savage bolshevists
To burn the world back to manure-good ash,
Wouldn't I stick the salvia in my coat!
But these themselves must burn, these louts!

The dragon-faced,
The anger-reddened, golden-throated salvia
With its long antennæ of rage put out
Upon the frightened air.
Ugh, how I love its fangs of perfect rage
That gnash the air;
The molten gold of its intolerable rage
Hot in the throat.

I long to be a bolshevist
And set the stinking rubbish-heap of this foul world
Afire at a myriad scarlet points,
A bolshevist, a salvia-face
To lick the world with flame that licks it clean.
I long to see its chock-full crowdedness
And glutted squirming populousness on fire
Like a field of filthy weeds
Burnt back to ash,
And then to see the new, real souls sprout up.

Not this vast rotting cabbage patch we call the world;
But from the ash-scarred fallow
New wild souls.

Nettles, and a rose sprout,
Hibiscus, and mere grass,
Salvia still in a rage
And almond honey-still,
And fig-wort stinking for the carrion wasp;
All the lot of them, and let them fight it out.

But not a trace of foul equality,
Nor sound of still more foul human perfection.
You need not clear the world like a cabbage patch for me;
Leave me my nettles,
Let me fight the wicked, obstreperous weeds myself, and put
    them in their place,
Severely in their place.
I don't at all want to annihilate them,
I like a row with them,
But I won't be put on a cabbage-idealistic level of equality
    with them.

What rot, to see the cabbage and hibiscus-tree
As equals!
What rot, to say the louts along the Corso
In Sunday suits and yellow shoes
Are my equals!
I am their superior, saluting the hibiscus flower, not them.
The same I say to the profiteers from the hotels, the
    money-fat-ones,
Profiteers here being called dog-fish, stinking dog-fish,
    sharks.
The same I say to the pale and elegant persons,
Pale-face authorities loitering tepidly:
That I salute the red hibiscus flowers
And send mankind to its inferior blazes.
Mankind's inferior blazes,
And these along with it, all the inferior lot—
These bolshevists,
These dog-fish,

These precious and ideal ones,
All rubbish ready for fire.

And I salute hibiscus and the salvia flower
Upon the breasts of loutish bolshevists,
Damned loutish bolshevists,
Who perhaps will do the business after all,
In the long run, in spite of themselves.

Meanwhile, alas
For me no fellow-men,
No salvia-frenzied comrades, antennæ
Of yellow-red, outreaching, living wrath
Upon the smouldering air,
And throat of brimstone-molten angry gold.
Red, angry men are a race extinct, alas!

Never
To be a bolshevist
With a hibiscus flower behind my ear
In sign of life, of lovely, dangerous life
And passionate disquality of men;
In sign of dauntless, silent violets,
And impudent nettles grabbing the under-earth,
And cabbages born to be cut and eat,
And salvia fierce to crow and shout for fight,
And rosy-red hibiscus wincingly
Unfolding all her coiled and lovely self
In a doubtful world.

Never, bolshevistically
To be able to stand for all these!
Alas, alas, I have got to leave it all
To the youths in Sunday suits and yellow shoes
Who have pulled down the salvia flowers
And rosy delicate hibiscus flowers
And everything else to their disgusting level,
Never, of course, to put anything up again.

But yet
If they pull all the world down,
The process will amount to the same in the end.
Instead of flame and flame-clean ash,
Slow watery rotting back to level muck
And final humus,
Whence the re-start.

And still I cannot bear it
That they take hibiscus and the salvia flower.

   Taormina

The Evangelistic Beasts

Oh put them back, put them back in the four corners of the
heavens, where they belong, the Apocalyptic beasts. For with
their wings full of stars they rule the night, and man that
watches through the night lives four lives, and man that sleeps
through the night sleeps four sleeps, the sleep of the lion, the
sleep of the bull, the sleep of the man, and the eagle's sleep. After
which the lion wakes, and it is day. Then from the four quarters
the four winds blow, and life has its changes. But when the
heavens are empty, empty of the four great Beasts, the four
Natures, the four Winds, the four Quarters, then sleep is empty
too, man sleeps no more like the lion and the bull, nor wakes
from the light-eyed eagle sleep.

St Matthew

They are not all beasts.
One is a man, for example, and one is a bird.

I, Matthew, am a man.

'And I, if I be lifted up, will draw all men unto me' –

That is Jesus.
But then Jesus was not quite a man.
He was the Son of Man
Filius Meus, O remorseless logic
Out of His own mouth.

I, Matthew, being a man
Cannot be lifted up, the Paraclete
To draw all men unto me,
Seeing I am on a par with all men.

I, on the other hand,
Am drawn to the Uplifted, as all men are drawn,
To the Son of Man
Filius Meus.

Wilt thou lift me up, Son of Man?
How my heart beats!
I am man.

I am man, and therefore my heart beats, and throws the dark
    blood from side to side
All the time I am lifted up.
Yes, even during my uplifting.

And if it ceased?
If it ceased, I should be no longer man
As I am, if my heart in uplifting ceased to beat, to toss the dark
    blood from side to side, causing my myriad secret streams.

After the cessation
I might be a soul in bliss, an angel, approximating to the
    Uplifted;
But that is another matter;
I am Matthew, the man,
And I am not that other angelic matter.

So I will be lifted up, Saviour,
But put me down again in time, Master,
Before my heart stops beating, and I become what I am not.
Put me down again on the earth, Jesus, on the brown soil
Where flowers sprout in the acrid humus, and fade into
    humus again.
Where beasts drop their unlicked young, and pasture, and
    drop their droppings among the turf.
Where the adder darts horizontal.
Down on the damp, unceasing ground, where my feet
    belong
And even my heart, Lord, forever, after all uplifting:
The crumbling, damp, fresh land, life horizontal and ceaseless.

Matthew I am, the man.
And I take the wings of the morning, to Thee, Crucified,
    Glorified.
But while flowers club their petals at evening
And rabbits make pills among the short grass
And long snakes quickly glide into the dark hole in the wall,
    hearing man approach,
I must be put down, Lord, in the afternoon,
And at evening I must leave off my wings of the spirit
As I leave off my braces,
And I must resume my nakedness like a fish, sinking down the
    dark reversion of night
Like a fish seeking the bottom, Jesus,
ΙΧΘΥΣ
Face downwards
Veering slowly

66

Down between the steep slopes of darkness, fucus-dark,
    seaweed-fringed valleys of the waters under the sea,
Over the edge of the soundless cataract
Into the fathomless, bottomless pit
Where my soul falls in the last throes of bottomless
    convulsion, and is fallen
Utterly beyond Thee, Dove of the Spirit;
Beyond everything, except itself.

Nay, Son of Man, I have been lifted up.
To Thee I rose like a rocket ending in mid-heaven.
But even thou, Son of Man, canst not quaff out the dregs of
    terrestrial manhood!
They fall back from Thee.

They fall back, and like a dripping of quicksilver taking the
    downward track,
Break into drops, burn into drops of blood, and dropping,
    dropping take wing
Membraned, blood-veined wings.
On fans of unsuspected tissue, like bats
They thread and thrill and flicker ever downward
To the dark zenith of Thine antipodes
Jesus Uplifted.

Bat-winged heart of man,
Reversed flame
Shuddering a strange way down the bottomless pit
To the great depths of its reversèd zenith.

Afterwards, afterwards
Morning comes, and I shake the dews of night from the wings
    of my spirit
And mount like a lark, Beloved.

But remember, Saviour,
That my heart which like a lark at heaven's gate singing,
    hovers morning-bright to Thee,

Throws still the dark blood back and forth
In the avenues where the bat hangs sleeping, upside-down
And to me undeniable, Jesus.

Listen, Paraclete.
I can no more deny the bat-wings of my fathom-flickering
    spirit of darkness
Than the wings of the Morning and Thee, Thou Glorified.

I am Matthew, the Man:
It is understood.
And Thou art Jesus, Son of Man
Drawing all men unto Thee, but bound to release them when
    the hour strikes.

I have been, and I have returned.
I have mounted up on the wings of the morning, and I have
    dredged down to the zenith's reversal.
Which is my way, being man.
Gods may stay in mid-heaven, the Son of Man has climbed to
    the Whitsun zenith,
But I, Matthew, being a man
Am a traveller back and forth.

So be it.

The Mosquito

When did you start your tricks,
Monsieur?

What do you stand on such high legs for?
Why this length of shredded shank,
You exaltation?

Is it so that you shall lift your centre of gravity upwards
And weigh no more than air as you alight upon me,
Stand upon me weightless, you phantom?

I heard a woman call you the Winged Victory
In sluggish Venice.
You turn your head towards your tail, and smile.

How can you put so much devilry
Into that translucent phantom shred
Of a frail corpus?

Queer, with your thin wings and your streaming legs,
How you sail like a heron, or a dull clot of air,
A nothingness.

Yet what an aura surrounds you;
Your evil little aura, prowling, and casting a numbness on my
      mind.

That is your trick, your bit of filthy magic:
Invisibility, and the anæsthetic power
To deaden my attention in your direction.

But I know your game now, streaky sorcerer.
Queer, how you stalk and prowl the air
In circles and evasions, enveloping me,
Ghoul on wings
Winged Victory.

Settle, and stand on long thin shanks
Eyeing me sideways, and cunningly conscious that I am aware,
You speck.

I hate the way you lurch off sideways into air
Having read my thoughts against you.

Come then, let us play at unawares,
And see who wins in this sly game of bluff.
Man or mosquito.

You don't know that I exist, and I don't know that you exist.
Now then!

It is your trump,
It is your hateful little trump,
You pointed fiend,
Which shakes my sudden blood to hatred of you:
It is your small, high, hateful bugle in my ear.

Why do you do it?
Surely it is bad policy.

They say you can't help it.

If that is so, then I believe a little in Providence protecting the
    innocent.
But it sounds so amazingly like a slogan,
A yell of triumph as you snatch my scalp.

Blood, red blood
Super-magical
Forbidden liquor.

I behold you stand
For a second enspasmed in oblivion,
Obscenely ecstasied
Sucking live blood,
My blood.

Such silence, such suspended transport,
Such gorging,
Such obscenity of trespass.

You stagger
As well as you may.
Only your accursed hairy frailty,
Your own imponderable weightlessness
Saves you, wafts you away on the very draught my anger
    makes in its snatching.

Away with a pæan of derision,
You winged blood-drop.

Can I not overtake you?
Are you one too many for me,
Winged Victory?
Am I not mosquito enough to out-mosquito you?

Queer, what a big stain my sucked blood makes
Beside the infinitesimal faint smear of you!
Queer, what a dim dark smudge you have disappeared into!

Siracusa

Fish

Fish, oh Fish,
So little matters!

Whether the waters rise and cover the earth
Or whether the waters wilt in the hollow places.
All one to you.

Aqueous, subaqueous,
Submerged
And wave-thrilled.

As the waters roll
Roll you.
The waters wash,
You wash in oneness
And never emerge.

Never know,
Never grasp.

Your life a sluice of sensation along your sides,
A flush at the flails of your fins, down the whorl of your
    tail,
And water wetly on fire in the grates of your gills;
Fixed water-eyes.

Even snakes lie together.

But oh, fish, that rock in water,
You lie only with the waters;
One touch.
No fingers, no hands and feet, no lips;
No tender muzzles,
No wistful bellies,
No loins of desire,
None.

You and the naked element,
Sway-wave.
Curvetting bits of tin in the evening light.

Who is it ejects his sperm to the naked flood?
In the wave-mother?
Who swims enwombed?
Who lies with the waters of his silent passion, womb-element?
– Fish in the waters under the earth.

What price *his* bread upon the waters?
Himself all silvery himself
In the element,
No more.

Nothing more.

Himself,
And the element.
Food, of course!
Water-eager eyes,
Mouth-gate open
And strong spine urging, driving;
And desirous belly gulping.

Fear also!
He knows fear!
Water-eyes craning,
A rush that almost screams,
Almost fish-voice
As the pike comes . . .
Then gay fear, that turns the tail sprightly, from a shadow.

Food, and fear, and joie de vivre,
Without love.

The other way about:
Joie de vivre, and fear, and food,
All without love.

Quelle joie de vivre
Dans l'eau!
Slowly to gape through the waters,
Alone with the element;
To sink, and rise, and go to sleep with the waters;
To speak endless inaudible wavelets into the wave;
To breathe from the flood at the gills,
Fish-blood slowly running next to the flood, extracting
    fish-fire:
To have the element under one, like a lover;
And to spring away with a curvetting click in the air,
Provocative.
Dropping back with a slap on the face of the flood.
And merging oneself!

To be a fish!

So utterly without misgiving
To be a fish
In the waters.

Loveless, and so lively!
Born before God was love,
Or life knew loving.
Beautifully beforehand with it all.

Admitted, they swarm in companies,
Fishes.
They drive in shoals.
But soundless, and out of contact.
They exchange no word, no spasm, not even anger.
Not one touch.
Many suspended together, forever apart,
Each one alone with the waters, upon one wave with the rest.

A magnetism in the water between them only.

I saw a water-serpent swim across the Anapo,
And I said to my heart, *look, look at him!*

With his head up, steering like a bird!
He's a rare one, but he belongs . . .

But sitting in a boat on the Zeller lake
And watching the fishes in the breathing waters
Lift and swim and go their way—

I said to my heart, *who are these?*
And my heart couldn't own them . . .

A slim young pike, with smart fins
And grey-striped suit, a young cub of a pike
Slouching along away below, half out of sight,
Like a lout on an obscure pavement . . .

Aha, there's somebody in the know!

But watching closer
That motionless deadly motion,
That unnatural barrel body, that long ghoul nose . . .
I left off hailing him.

I had made a mistake, I didn't know him,
This grey, monotonous soul in the water,
This intense individual in shadow,
Fish-alive.

I didn't know his God.
I didn't know his God.

Which is perhaps the last admission that life has to wring out
of us.

I saw, dimly,
Once a big pike rush,
And small fish fly like splinters.
And I said to my heart, *there are limits*
To you, my heart;
And to the one God.
Fish are beyond me.

Other Gods
Beyond my range . . . gods beyond my God . . .

They are beyond me, are fishes.
I stand at the pale of my being
And look beyond, and see
Fish, in the outerwards,
As one stands on a bank and looks in.

I have waited with a long rod
And suddenly pulled a gold-and-greenish, lucent fish from
    below,
And had him fly like a halo round my head,
Lunging in the air on the line.

Unhooked his gorping, water-horny mouth,
And seen his horror-tilted eye,
His red-gold, water-precious, mirror-flat bright eye;
And felt him beat in my hand, with his mucous, leaping
life-throb.
And my heart accused itself
Thinking: *I am not the measure of creation.*
This is beyond me, this fish.
His God stands outside my God.

And the gold-and-green pure lacquer-mucus comes off in my
    hand,
And the red-gold mirror-eye stares and dies,
And the water-suave contour dims.

But not before I have had to know
He was born in front of my sunrise,
Before my day.

He outstarts me.
And I, a many-fingered horror of daylight to him,
Have made him die.

Fishes
With their gold, red eyes, and green-pure gleam, and
    under-gold,
And their pre-world loneliness,
And more-than-lovelessness,
And white meat;
They move in other circles.

Outsiders.
Water-wayfarers.
Things of one element.
Aqueous,
Each by itself.

Cats, and the Neapolitans,
Sulphur sun-beasts,
Thirst for fish as for more-than-water;
Water-alive
To quench their over-sulphureous lusts.

But I, I only wonder
And don't know.
I don't know fishes.

In the beginning
Jesus was called The Fish. . . .
And in the end.

    Zell-am-See

Bat

At evening, sitting on this terrace,
When the sun from the west, beyond Pisa, beyond the
    mountains of Carrara
Departs, and the world is taken by surprise . . .

When the tired flower of Florence is in gloom beneath the
    glowing
Brown hills surrounding . . .

When under the arches of the Ponte Vecchio
A green light enters against stream, flush from the west,
Against the current of obscure Arno . . .

Look up, and you see things flying
Between the day and the night;
Swallows with spools of dark thread sewing the shadows
    together.

A circle swoop, and a quick parabola under the bridge
    arches
Where light pushes through;
A sudden turning upon itself of a thing in the air.
A dip to the water.

And you think:
'The swallows are flying so late!'

Swallows?

Dark air-life looping
Yet missing the pure loop . . .
A twitch, a twitter, an elastic shudder in flight
And serrated wings against the sky,
Like a glove, a black glove thrown up at the light,
And falling back.

Never swallows!
Bats!
The swallows are gone.

At a wavering instant the swallows give way to bats
By the Ponte Vecchio . . .
Changing guard.

Bats, and an uneasy creeping in one's scalp
As the bats swoop overhead!
Flying madly.

Pipistrello!
Black piper on an infinitesimal pipe.
Little lumps that fly in air and have voices indefinite, wildly
    vindictive;

Wings like bits of umbrella.

Bats!

Creatures that hang themselves up like an old rag, to sleep;
And disgustingly upside down.
Hanging upside down like rows of disgusting old rags
And grinning in their sleep.
Bats!

In China the bat is symbol of happiness.

Not for me!

Man and Bat

When I went into my room, at mid-morning,
Say ten o'clock . . .
My room, a crash-box over that great stone rattle
The Via de' Bardi. . . .

When I went into my room at mid-morning,
Why? . . . a bird!

A bird
Flying round the room in insane circles.

In insane circles!
. . . A bat!

A disgusting bat
At mid-morning! . . .

Out! Go out!

Round and round and round
With a twitchy, nervous, intolerable flight,
And a neurasthenic lunge,
And an impure frenzy;
A bat, big as a swallow.

Out, out of my room!

The venetian shutters I push wide
To the free, calm upper air;
Loop back the curtains . . .

Now out, out from my room!

So to drive him out, flicking with my white handkerchief: *Go!*
But he will not.

Round and round and round
In an impure haste,

Fumbling, a beast in air,
And stumbling, lunging and touching the walls, the
    bell-wires
About my room!

Always refusing to go out into the air
Above that crash-gulf of the Via de' Bardi,
Yet blind with frenzy, with cluttered fear.

At last he swerved into the window bay,
But blew back, as if an incoming wind blew him in again.
A strong inrushing wind.

And round and round and round!
Blundering more insane, and leaping, in throbs, to clutch at a
    corner,
At a wire, at a bell-rope:
On and on, watched relentless by me, round and round in my
    room,
Round and round and dithering with tiredness and haste and
    increasing delirium
Flicker-splashing round my room.

I would not let him rest;
Not one instant cleave, cling like a blot with his breast to the
    wall
In an obscure corner.
Not an instant!

I flicked him on,
Trying to drive him through the window.
Again he swerved into the window bay
And I ran forward, to frighten him forth.
But he rose, and from a terror worse than me he flew past me
Back into my room, and round, round, round in my room
Clutch, cleave, stagger,
Dropping about the air
Getting tired.

Something seemed to blow him back from the window
Every time he swerved at it;
Back on a strange parabola, then round, round, dizzy in my
    room.

He *could* not go out,
I also realised . . .
It was the light of day which he could not enter,
Any more than I could enter the white-hot door of a blast
    furnace.

He could not plunge into the daylight that streamed at the
    window.
It was asking too much of his nature.

Worse even than the hideous terror of me with my
    handkerchief
Saying: *out, go out!* . . .
Was the horror of white daylight in the window!

So I switched on the electric light, thinking: *Now*
The outside will seem brown . . .

But no.
The outside did not seem brown.
And he did not mind the yellow electric light.

Silent!
He was having a silent rest.
But never!
Not in my room.

Round and round and round
Near the ceiling as if in a web,
Staggering;
Plunging, falling out of the web,
Broken in heaviness,
Lunging blindly,
Heavier;

And clutching, clutching for one second's pause,
Always, as if for one drop of rest,
One little drop.

And I!
Never, I say. . . .
Get out!

Flying slower,
Seeming to stumble, to fall in air,
Blind-weary.

Yet never able to pass the whiteness of light into freedom . . .
A bird would have dashed through, come what might.

Fall, sink, lurch, and round and round
Flicker, flicker-heavy;
Even wings heavy:
And cleave in a high corner for a second, like a clot, also a
    prayer.

But no.
Out, you beast.

Till he fell in a corner, palpitating, spent.
And there, a clot, he squatted and looked at me.
With sticking-out, bead-berry eyes, black,
And improper derisive ears,
And shut wings,
And brown, furry body.

Brown, nut-brown, fine fur!
But it might as well have been hair on a spider; thing
With long, black-paper ears.

So, a dilemma!
He squatted there like something unclean.

No, he must not squat, nor hang, obscene, in my room!

Yet nothing on earth will give him courage to pass the sweet
    fire of day.

What then?
Hit him and kill him and throw him away?

Nay,
I didn't create him.
Let the God that created him be responsible for his death . . .
Only, in the bright day, I will not have this clot in my room.

Let the God who is maker of bats watch with them in their
    unclean corners . . .
I admit a God in every crevice,
But not bats in my room;
Nor the God of bats, while the sun shines.

So out, out, you brute! . . .
And he lunged, flight-heavy, away from me, sideways, *a
    sghembo!*
And round and round and round my room, a clot with wings,
Impure even in weariness.

Wings dark skinny and flapping the air,
Lost their flicker.
Spent.

He fell again with a little thud
Near the curtain on the floor.
And there lay.

Ah death, death
You are no solution!
Bats must be bats.
Only life has a way out.
And the human soul is fated to wide-eyed responsibility
In life.

So I picked him up in a flannel jacket,
Well covered, lest he should bite me.

For I would have had to kill him if he'd bitten me, the impure
   one . . .
And he hardly stirred in my hand, muffled up.

Hastily, I shook him out of the window.

And away he went!
Fear craven in his tail.
Great haste, and straight, almost bird straight above the Via
   de' Bardi.
Above that crash-gulf of exploding whips,
Towards the Borgo San Jacopo.

And now, at evening, as he flickers over the river
Dipping with petty triumphant flight, and tittering over the
   sun's departure,
I believe he chirps, pipistrello, seeing me here on this terrace
   writing:
There he sits, the long loud one!
But I am greater than he . . .
I escaped him. . . .

   Florence

Snake

A snake came to my water-trough
On a hot, hot day, and I in pyjamas for the heat,
To drink there.

In the deep, strange-scented shade of the great dark carob-tree
I came down the steps with my pitcher
And must wait, must stand and wait, for there he was at the
    trough before me.

He reached down from a fissure in the earth-wall in the
    gloom
And trailed his yellow-brown slackness soft-bellied down,
    over the edge of the stone trough
And rested his throat upon the stone bottom,
And where the water had dripped from the tap, in a small
    clearness,
He sipped with his straight mouth,
Softly drank through his straight gums, into his slack long
    body,
Silently.

Someone was before me at my water-trough,
And I, like a second comer, waiting.

He lifted his head from his drinking, as cattle do,
And looked at me vaguely, as drinking cattle do,
And flickered his two-forked tongue from his lips, and mused
    a moment,
And stooped and drank a little more,
Being earth-brown, earth-golden from the burning bowels of
    the earth
On the day of Sicilian July, with Etna smoking.

The voice of my education said to me
He must be killed,

For in Sicily the black, black snakes are innocent, the gold are
  venomous.

And voices in me said, If you were a man
You would take a stick and break him now, and finish him off.

But must I confess how I liked him,
How glad I was he had come like a guest in quiet, to drink at
  my water-trough
And depart peaceful, pacified, and thankless,
Into the burning bowels of this earth?

Was it cowardice, that I dared not kill him?
Was it perversity, that I longed to talk to him?
Was it humility, to feel so honoured?
I felt so honoured.

And yet those voices:
If you were not afraid, you would kill him!

And truly I was afraid, I was most afraid,
But even so, honoured still more
That he should seek my hospitality
From out the dark door of the secret earth.

He drank enough
And lifted his head, dreamily, as one who has drunken,
And flickered his tongue like a forked night on the air, so black,
Seeming to lick his lips,
And looked around like a god, unseeing, into the air,
And slowly turned his head,
And slowly, very slowly, as if thrice adream,
Proceeded to draw his slow length curving round
And climb again the broken bank of my wall-face.
And as he put his head into that dreadful hole,
And as he slowly drew up, snake-easing his shoulders, and
  entered farther,
A sort of horror, a sort of protest against his withdrawing into
  that horrid black hole,

Deliberately going into the blackness, and slowly drawing
    himself after,
Overcame me now his back was turned.

I looked round, I put down my pitcher,
I picked up a clumsy log
And threw it at the water-trough with a clatter.

I think it did not hit him,
But suddenly that part of him that was left behind convulsed
    in undignified haste,
Writhed like lightning, and was gone
Into the black hole, the earth-lipped fissure in the wall-front,
At which, in the intense still noon, I stared with fascination.

And immediately I regretted it.
I thought how paltry, how vulgar, what a mean act!
I despised myself and the voices of my accursed human
    education.

And I thought of the albatross,
And I wished he would come back, my snake.

For he seemed to me again like a king,
Like a king in exile, uncrowned in the underworld,
Now due to be crowned again.

And so, I missed my chance with one of the lords
Of life.
And I have something to expiate;
A pettiness.

    Taormina

Baby Tortoise

You know what it is to be born alone,
Baby tortoise!

The first day to heave your feet little by little from the shell,
Not yet awake,
And remain lapsed on earth,
Not quite alive.

A tiny, fragile, half-animate bean.

To open your tiny beak-mouth, that looks as if it would never
    open,
Like some iron door;
To lift the upper hawk-beak from the lower base
And reach your skinny little neck
And take your first bite at some dim bit of herbage,
Alone, small insect,
Tiny bright-eye,
Slow one.

To take your first solitary bite
And move on your slow, solitary hunt.
Your bright, dark little eye,
Your eye of a dark disturbed night,
Under its slow lid, tiny baby tortoise,
So indomitable.

No one ever heard you complain.

You draw your head forward, slowly, from your little wimple
And set forward, slow-dragging, on your four-pinned toes,
Rowing slowly forward.
Whither away, small bird?
Rather like a baby working its limbs,
Except that you make slow, ageless progress
And a baby makes none.

The touch of sun excites you,
And the long ages, and the lingering chill
Make you pause to yawn,
Opening your impervious mouth,
Suddenly beak-shaped, and very wide, like some suddenly
    gaping pincers;
Soft red tongue, and hard thin gums,
Then close the wedge of your little mountain front,
Your face, baby tortoise.

Do you wonder at the world, as slowly you turn your head in
    its wimple
And look with laconic, black eyes?
Or is sleep coming over you again,
The non-life?

You are so hard to wake.

Are you able to wonder?
Or is it just your indomitable will and pride of the first life
Looking round
And slowly pitching itself against the inertia
Which had seemed invincible?

The vast inanimate,
And the fine brilliance of your so tiny eye,
Challenger.

Nay, tiny shell-bird,
What a huge vast inanimate it is, that you must row against,
What an incalculable inertia.

Challenger,
Little Ulysses, fore-runner,
No bigger than my thumb-nail,
Buon viaggio,

All animate creation on your shoulder,
Set forth, little Titan, under your battle-shield.

The ponderous, preponderate,
Inanimate universe;
And you are slowly moving, pioneer, you alone.

How vivid your travelling seems now, in the troubled
    sunshine,
Stoic, Ulyssean atom;
Suddenly hasty, reckless, on high toes.

Voiceless little bird,
Resting your head half out of your wimple
In the slow dignity of your eternal pause.
Alone, with no sense of being alone,
And hence six times more solitary;
Fulfilled of the slow passion of pitching through immemorial
    ages
Your little round house in the midst of chaos.

Over the garden earth,
Small bird,
Over the edge of all things.

Traveller,
With your tail tucked a little on one side
Like a gentleman in a long-skirted coat.

All life carried on your shoulder,
Invincible fore-runner.

Tortoise Shell

The Cross, the Cross
Goes deeper in than we know,
Deeper into life;
Right into the marrow
And through the bone.
Along the back of the baby tortoise
The scales are locked in an arch like a bridge,
Scale-lapping, like a lobster's sections
Or a bee's.

Then crossways down his sides
Tiger-stripes and wasp-bands.

Five, and five again, and five again,
And round the edges twenty-five little ones,
The sections of the baby tortoise shell.

Four, and a keystone;
Four, and a keystone;
Four, and a keystone;
Then twenty-four, and a tiny little keystone.

It needed Pythagoras to see life playing with counters on the
    living back
Of the baby tortoise;
Life establishing the first eternal mathematical tablet,
Not in stone, like the Judean Lord, or bronze, but in
    life-clouded, life-rosy tortoise shell.

The first little mathematical gentleman
Stepping, wee mite, in his loose trousers
Under all the eternal dome of mathematical law.

Fives, and tens,
Threes and fours and twelves,

All the *volte face* of decimals,
The whirligig of dozens and the pinnacle of seven.

Turn him on his back,
The kicking little beetle,
And there again, on his shell-tender, earth-touching belly,
The long cleavage of division, upright of the eternal cross
And on either side count five,
On each side, two above, on each side, two below
The dark bar horizontal.

The Cross!
It goes right through him, the sprottling insect,
Through his cross-wise cloven psyche,
Through his five-fold complex-nature.

So turn him over on his toes again;
Four pin-point toes, and a problematical thumb-piece,
Four rowing limbs, and one wedge-balancing head,
Four and one makes five, which is the clue to all mathematics.

The Lord wrote it all down on the little slate
Of the baby tortoise.
Outward and visible indication of the plan within,
The complex, manifold involvedness of an individual creature
Plotted out
On this small bird, this rudiment,
This little dome, this pediment
Of all creation,
This slow one.

Lui et Elle

She is large and matronly
And rather dirty,
A little sardonic-looking, as if domesticity had driven her
    to it.

Though what she does, except lay four eggs at random in the
    garden once a year
And put up with her husband,
I don't know.

She likes to eat.
She hurries up, striding reared on long uncanny legs
When food is going.
Oh yes, she can make haste when she likes.

She snaps the soft bread from my hand in great mouthfuls,
Opening her rather pretty wedge of an iron, pristine face
Into an enormously wide-beaked mouth
Like sudden curved scissors,
And gulping at more than she can swallow, and working her
    thick, soft tongue,
And having the bread hanging over her chin.

O Mistress, Mistress,
Reptile mistress,
Your eye is very dark, very bright,
And it never softens
Although you watch.

She knows,
She knows well enough to come for food,
Yet she sees me not;
Her bright eye sees, but not me, not anything,
Sightful, sightless, seeing and visionless,
Reptile mistress.

94

Taking bread in her curved, gaping, toothless mouth,
She has no qualm when she catches my finger in her steel
overlapping gums,
But she hangs on, and my shout and my shrinking are
nothing to her.
She does not even know she is nipping me with her curved
beak.
Snake-like she draws at my finger, while I drag it in horror
away.

Mistress, reptile mistress,
You are almost too large, I am almost frightened.

He is much smaller,
Dapper beside her,
And ridiculously small.

Her laconic eye has an earthy, materialistic look,
His, poor darling, is almost fiery.
His wimple, his blunt-prowed face,
His low forehead, his skinny neck, his long, scaled, striving legs,
So striving, striving,
Are all more delicate than she,
And he has a cruel scar on his shell.

Poor darling, biting at her feet,
Running beside her like a dog, biting her earthy, splay feet,
Nipping her ankles,
Which she drags apathetic away, though without retreating
into her shell.

Agelessly silent,
And with a grim, reptile determination,
Cold, voiceless age-after-age behind him, serpents' long
obstinacy
Of horizontal persistence.

Little old man
Scuffling beside her, bending down, catching his opportunity,

Parting his steel-trap face, so suddenly, and seizing her scaly
  ankle,
And hanging grimly on,
Letting go at last as she drags away,
And closing his steel-trap face.

His steel-trap, stoic, ageless, handsome face.
Alas, what a fool he looks in this scuffle.

And how he feels it!
The lonely rambler, the stoic, dignified stalker through chaos,
The immune, the animate,
Enveloped in isolation,
Fore-runner.
Now look at him!

Alas, the spear is through the side of his isolation.
His adolescence saw him crucified into sex,
Doomed, in the long crucifixion of desire, to seek his
  consummation beyond himself.
Divided into passionate duality,
He, so finished and immune, now broken into desirous
  fragmentariness,
Doomed to make an intolerable fool of himself
In his effort toward completion again.

Poor little earthy house-inhabiting Osiris,
The mysterious bull tore him at adolescence into pieces,
And he must struggle after reconstruction, ignominiously.

And so behold him following the tail
Of that mud-hovel of his slowly rambling spouse,
Like some unhappy bull at the tail of a cow,
But with more than bovine, grim, earth-dank persistence.

Suddenly seizing the ugly ankle as she stretches out to walk,
Roaming over the sods,
Or, if it happen to show, at her pointed, heavy tail
Beneath the low-dropping back-board of her shell.

Their two shells like domed boats bumping,
Hers huge, his small;
Their splay feet rambling and rowing like paddles,
And stumbling mixed up in one another,
In the race of love –
Two tortoises,
She huge, he small.

She seems earthily apathetic,
And he has a reptile's awful persistence.

I heard a woman pitying her, pitying the Mère Tortue.
While I, I pity Monsieur.
'He pesters her and torments her,' said the woman.
How much more is *he* pestered and tormented, say I.
What can he do?
He is dumb, he is visionless,
Conceptionless.
His black, sad-lidded eye sees but beholds not
As her earthen mound moves on.
But he catches the folds of vulnerable, leathery skin,
Nail-studded, that shake beneath her shell,
And drags at these with his beak,
Drags and drags and bites,
While she pulls herself free, and rows her dull mound along.

Tortoise Gallantry

Making his advances
He does not look at her, nor sniff at her,
No, not even sniff at her, his nose is blank.

Only he senses the vulnerable folds of skin
That work beneath her while she sprawls along
In her ungainly pace,
Her folds of skin that work and row
Beneath the earth-soiled hovel in which she moves.

And so he strains beneath her housey walls
And catches her trouser-legs in his beak
Suddenly, or her skinny limb,
And strange and grimly drags at her
Like a dog,
Only agelessly silent, with a reptile's awful persistency.

Grim, gruesome gallantry, to which he is doomed.
Dragged out of an eternity of silent isolation
And doomed to partiality, partial being,
Ache, and want of being,
Want,
Self-exposure, hard humiliation, need to add himself on to her.

Born to walk alone,
Fore-runner,
Now suddenly distracted into this mazy side-track.
This awkward, harrowing pursuit,
This grim necessity from within.

Does she know
As she moves eternally slowly away?
Or is he driven against her with a bang, like a bird flying in
    the dark against a window,
All knowledgeless?

The awful concussion,
And the still more awful need to persist, to follow, follow,
    continue,

Driven, after æons of pristine, fore-god-like singleness and
    oneness,
At the end of some mysterious, red-hot iron,
Driven away from himself into her tracks,
Forced to crash against her.

Stiff, gallant, irascible, crook-legged reptile,
Little gentleman,
Sorry plight,
We ought to look the other way.

Save that, having come with you so far,
We will go on to the end.

Turkey-Cock

You ruffled black blossom,
You glossy dark wind.

Your sort of gorgeousness,
Dark and lustrous
And skinny repulsive
And poppy-glossy,
Is the gorgeousness that evokes my most puzzled admiration.

Your aboriginality
Deep, unexplained,
Like a Red Indian darkly unfinished and aloof,
Seems like the black and glossy seeds of countless centuries.

Your wattles are the colour of steel-slag which has been
    red-hot
And is going cold,
Cooling to a powdery, pale-oxydised sky-blue.

Why do you have wattles, and a naked, wattled head?
Why do you arch your naked-set eye with a more-than-
    comprehensible arrogance?

The vulture is bald, so is the condor, obscenely,
But only you have thrown this amazing mantilla of oxydised
    sky-blue
And hot red over you.

This queer dross shawl of blue and vermilion,
Whereas the peacock has a diadem.

I wonder why.
Perhaps it is a sort of uncanny decoration, a veil of loose skin.
Perhaps it is your assertion, in all this ostentation, of raw
    contradictoriness.
Your wattles drip down like a shawl to your breast

And the point of your mantilla drops across your nose,
    unpleasantly.
Or perhaps it is something unfinished
A bit of slag still adhering, after your firing in the furnace of
    creation.

Or perhaps there is something in your wattles of a bull's dew-lap
Which slips down like a pendulum to balance the throbbing
    mass of a generous breast,

The over-drip of a great passion hanging in the balance.
Only yours would be a raw, unsmelted passion, that will not
    quite fuse from the dross.

You contract yourself,
You arch yourself as an archer's bow
Which quivers indrawn as you clench your spine
Until your veiled head almost touches backward
To the root-rising of your erected tail.
And one intense and backward-curving frisson
Seizes you as you clench yourself together
Like some fierce magnet bringing its poles together.

Burning, pale positive pole of your wattled head!
And from the darkness of that opposite one
The upstart of your round-barred, sun-round tail!

Whilst between the two, along the tense arch of your back
Blows the magnetic current in fierce blasts,
Ruffling black, shining feathers like lifted mail,
Shuddering storm wind, or a water rushing through.

Your brittle, super-sensual arrogance
Tosses the crape of red across your brow and down your breast
As you draw yourself upon yourself in insistence.

It is a declaration of such tension in will
As time has not dared to avouch, nor eternity been able to
    unbend
Do what it may.

A raw American will, that has never been tempered by life;
You brittle, will-tense bird with a foolish eye.

The peacock lifts his rods of bronze
And struts blue-brilliant out of the far East.
But watch a turkey prancing low on earth
Drumming his vaulted wings, as savages drum
Their rhythms on long-drawn, hollow, sinister drums.
The ponderous, sombre sound of the great drum of
    Huichilobos
In pyramid Mexico, during sacrifice.

Drum, and the turkey onrush
Sudden, demonic dauntlessness, full abreast,
All the bronze gloss of all his myriad petals
Each one apart and instant.
Delicate frail crescent of the gentle outline of white
At each feather-tip
So delicate:
Yet the bronze wind-bell suddenly clashing
And the eye overweening into madness.

Turkey-cock, turkey-cock,
Are you the bird of the next dawn?

Has the peacock had his day, does he call in vain, screecher,
    for the sun to rise?
The eagle, the dove, and the barnyard rooster, do they call in
    vain, trying to wake the morrow?
And do you await us, wattled father, Westward?
Will your yell do it?

Take up the trail of the vanished American
Where it disappeared at the foot of the crucifix.
Take up the primordial Indian obstinacy,
The more than human, dense insistence of will,
And disdain, and blankness, and onrush, and prise open the
    new day with them?

The East a dead letter, and Europe moribund . . . Is that so?
And those sombre, dead, feather-lustrous Aztecs,
    Amerindians,
In all the sinister splendour of their red blood-sacrifices,
Do they stand under the dawn, half-godly, half-demon,
    awaiting the cry of the turkey-cock?
Or must you go through the fire once more, till you're smelted
    pure,
Slag-wattled turkey-cock,
Dross-jabot?

    Fiesole

The Blue Jay

The blue jay with a crest on his head
Comes round the cabin in the snow.
He runs in the snow like a bit of blue metal,
Turning his back on everything.

From the pine-tree that towers and hisses like a pillar of
    shaggy cloud
Immense above the cabin
Comes a strident laugh as we approach, this little black dog
    and I.
So halts the little black bitch on four spread paws in the
    snow
And looks up inquiringly into the pillar of cloud,
With a tinge of misgiving.
Ca-a-a! comes the scrape of ridicule out of the tree.

What voice of the Lord is that, from the tree of smoke?

Oh, Bibbles, little black bitch in the snow,
With a pinch of snow in the groove of your silly snub nose,
What do you look at *me* for?
What do you look at me for, with such misgiving?

It's the blue jay laughing at us.
It's the blue jay jeering at us, Bibs.

Every day since the snow is here
The blue jay paces round the cabin, very busy, picking up
    bits,
Turning his back on us all,
And bobbing his thick dark crest about the snow, as if darkly
    saying:
I ignore those folk who look out.

You acid-blue metallic bird,
You thick bird with a strong crest,

Who are you?
Whose boss are you, with all your bully way?
You copper-sulphate blue bird!

   Lobo

Kangaroo

In the northern hemisphere
Life seems to leap at the air, or skim under the wind
Like stags on rocky ground, or pawing horses, or springy
    scut-tailed rabbits.

Or else rush horizontal to charge at the sky's horizon,
Like bulls or bisons or wild pigs.

Or slip like water slippery towards its ends,
As foxes, stoats, and wolves, and prairie dogs.

Only mice, and moles, and rats, and badgers, and beavers, and
    perhaps bears
Seem belly-plumbed to the earth's mid-navel.
Or frogs that when they leap come flop, and flop to the centre
    of the earth.

But the yellow antipodal Kangaroo, when she sits up,
Who can unseat her, like a liquid drop that is heavy, and just
    touches earth.
The downward drip
The down-urge.
So much denser than cold-blooded frogs.

Delicate mother Kangaroo
Sitting up there rabbit-wise, but huge, plumb-weighted,
And lifting her beautiful slender face, oh! so much more
    gently and finely lined than a rabbit's, or than a hare's,
Lifting her face to nibble at a round white peppermint drop,
    which she loves, sensitive mother Kangaroo.

Her sensitive, long, pure-bred face.
Her full antipodal eyes, so dark,
So big and quiet and remote, having watched so many empty
    dawns in silent Australia.

Her little loose hands, and drooping Victorian shoulders.
And then her great weight below the waist, her vast pale belly
With a thin young yellow little paw hanging out, and straggle
    of a long thin ear, like ribbon,
Like a funny trimming to the middle of her belly, thin little
    dangle of an immature paw, and one thin ear.

Her belly, her big haunches
And, in addition, the great muscular python-stretch of her tail.

There, she shan't have any more peppermint drops.
So she wistfully, sensitively sniffs the air, and then turns, goes
    off in slow sad leaps

On the long flat skis of her legs,
Steered and propelled by that steel-strong snake of a tail.

Stops again, half turns, inquisitive to look back.
While something stirs quickly in her belly, and a lean little
    face comes out, as from a window,
Peaked and a bit dismayed,
Only to disappear again quickly away from the sight of the
    world, to snuggle down in the warmth,
Leaving the trail of a different paw hanging out.

Still she watches with eternal, cocked wistfulness!
How full her eyes are, like the full, fathomless, shining eyes of
    an Australian black-boy
Who has been lost so many centuries on the margins of
    existence!

She watches with insatiable wistfulness.
Untold centuries of watching for something to come,
For a new signal from life, in that silent lost land of the South.

Where nothing bites but insects and snakes and the sun, small
    life.
Where no bull roared, no cow ever lowed, no stag cried, no
    leopard screeched, no lion coughed, no dog barked,

But all was silent save for parrots occasionally, in the haunted
   blue bush.

Wistfully watching, with wonderful liquid eyes.
And all her weight, all her blood, dripping sack-wise down
   towards the earth's centre,
And the live little-one taking in its paw at the door of her
   belly.

Leap then, and come down on the line that draws to the
   earth's deep, heavy centre.

   Sydney

Mountain Lion

Climbing through the January snow, into the Lobo canyon
Dark grow the spruce-trees, blue is the balsam, water sounds
    still unfrozen, and the trail is still evident.

Men!
Two men!
Men! The only animal in the world to fear!

They hesitate.
We hesitate.
They have a gun.
We have no gun.

Then we all advance, to meet.

Two Mexicans, strangers, emerging out of the dark and snow
    and inwardness of the Lobo valley.
What are they doing here on this vanishing trail?

What is he carrying?
Something yellow,
A deer?

Qué tiene, amigo?
León –

He smiles, foolishly, as if he were caught doing wrong.
And we smile, foolishly, as if we didn't know.
He is quite gentle and dark-faced.

It is a mountain lion,
A long, long slim cat, yellow like a lioness.
Dead.

He trapped her this morning, he says, smiling foolishly.

Lift up her face,
Her round, bright face, bright as frost.

Her round, fine-fashioned head, with two dead ears;
And stripes in the brilliant frost of her face, sharp, fine dark
rays,
Dark, keen, fine rays in the brilliant frost of her face.
Beautiful dead eyes.

Hermoso es!

They go out towards the open;
We go on into the gloom of Lobo.
And above the trees I found her lair,
A hole in the blood-orange brilliant rocks that stick up, a little
cave.
And bones, and twigs, and a perilous ascent.

So, she will never leap up that way again, with the yellow flash
of a mountain lion's long shoot!
And her bright striped frost-face will never watch any more,
out of the shadow of the cave in the blood-orange rock,
Above the trees of the Lobo dark valley-mouth!

Instead, I look out.
And out to the dim of the desert, like a dream, never real;
To the snow of the Sangre de Cristo mountains, the ice of the
mountains of Picoris,
And near across at the opposite steep of snow, green trees
motionless standing in snow, like a Christmas toy.

And I think in this empty world there was room for me and a
mountain lion.
And I think in the world beyond, how easily we might spare a
million or two of humans
And never miss them.
Yet what a gap in the world, the missing white frost-face of
that slim yellow mountain lion!

Lobo

Autumn at Taos

Over the rounded sides of the Rockies, the aspens of autumn,
The aspens of autumn,
Like yellow hair of a tigress brindled with pines.

Down on my hearth-rug of desert, sage of the mesa,
An ash-grey pelt
Of wolf all hairy and level, a wolf's wild pelt.

Trot-trot to the mottled foot-hills, cedar-mottled and piñon;
Did you ever see an otter?
Silvery-sided, fish-fanged, fierce-faced, whiskered, mottled.

When I trot my little pony through the aspen-trees of the
    canyon,
Behold me trotting at ease betwixt the slopes of the golden
Great and glistening-feathered legs of the hawk of Horus;
The golden hawk of Horus
Astride above me.

But under the pines
I go slowly
As under the hairy belly of a great black bear.

Glad to emerge and look back
On the yellow, pointed aspen-trees laid one on another like
    feathers,
Feather over feather on the breast of the great and golden
Hawk as I say of Horus.

Pleased to be out in the sage and the pine fish-dotted
    foot-hills,
Past the otter's whiskers,
On to the fur of the wolf-pelt that strews the plain.

And then to look back to the rounded sides of the squatting
    Rockies,

Tigress brindled with aspen,
Jaguar-splashed, puma-yellow, leopard-livid slopes of
    America.

Make big eyes, little pony,
At all these skins of wild beasts;
They won't hurt you.

Fangs and claws and talons and beaks and hawk-eyes
Are nerveless just now.
So be easy.

    Taos

112

The American Eagle

The dove of Liberty sat on an egg
And hatched another eagle.

But didn't disown the bird.

Down with all eagles! cooed the Dove.
And down all eagles began to flutter, reeling from their perches:
Eagles with two heads, eagles with one, presently eagles with
    none
Fell from the hooks and were dead.

Till the American Eagle was the only eagle left in the world.

Then it began to fidget, shifting from one leg to the other,
Trying to look like a pelican,
And plucking out of his plumage a few loose feathers to
    feather the nests of all
The new naked little republics come into the world.

But the feathers were, comparatively, a mere flea-bite.
And the bub-eagle that Liberty had hatched was growing a
    startling big bird
On the roof of the world;
A bit awkward, and with a funny squawk in his voice,
His mother Liberty trying always to teach him to coo
And him always ending with a yawp
Coo! Coo! Coo! Coo-ark! Coo-ark! Quark!! Quark!!
YAWP!!!

So he clears his throat, the young Cock-eagle!
Now if the lilies of France lick Solomon in all his glory;
And the leopard cannot change his spots;
Nor the British lion his appetite;
Neither can a young Cock-eagle sit simpering
With an olive-sprig in his mouth.

It's not his nature.

The big bird of the Amerindian being the eagle,
Red Men still stick themselves over with bits of his fluff,
And feel absolutely IT.

So better make up your mind, American Eagle,
Whether you're a sucking dove, *Roo – coo – ooo! Quark!
    Yawp!!*
Or a pelican
Handing out a few loose golden breast-feathers, at moulting
    time;
Or a sort of prosperity-gander
Fathering endless ten-dollar golden eggs.

Or whether it actually is an eagle you are,
With a Roman nose
And claws not made to shake hands with,
And a Me-Almighty eye.

The new Proud Republic
Based on the mystery of pride.
Overweening men, full of power of life, commanding a
    teeming obedience.

Eagle of the Rockies, bird of men that are masters,
Lifting the rabbit-blood of the myriads up into something
    splendid,
Leaving a few bones;
Opening great wings in the face of the sheep-faced ewe
Who is losing her lamb,
Drinking a little blood, and loosing another royalty unto the
    world.

Is that you, American Eagle?

Or are you the goose that lays the golden egg?
Which is just a stone to anyone asking for meat.

And are you going to go on for ever
Laying that golden egg,
That addled golden egg?

   Lobo

How Beastly the Bourgeois Is

How beastly the bourgeois is
especially the male of the species —

Presentable, eminently presentable —
shall I make you a present of him?

Isn't he handsome? Isn't he healthy? Isn't he a fine specimen?
Doesn't he look the fresh clean Englishman, outside?
Isn't it God's own image? tramping his thirty miles a day
after partridges, or a little rubber ball?
wouldn't you like to be like that, well off, and quite the thing?
Oh, but wait!
Let him meet a new emotion, let him be faced with another
    man's need,
let him come home to a bit of moral difficulty, let life face
    him with a new demand on his understanding
and then watch him go soggy, like a wet meringue.
Watch him turn into a mess, either a fool or a bully.
Just watch the display of him, confronted with a new demand
    on his intelligence,
a new life-demand.

How beastly the bourgeois is
especially the male of the species —

Nicely groomed, like a mushroom
standing there so sleek and erect and eyeable —
and like a fungus, living on the remains of bygone life
sucking his life out of the dead leaves of greater life than his
    own.

And even so, he's stale, he's been there too long.
Touch him, and you'll find he's all gone inside
just like an old mushroom, all wormy inside, and hollow
under a smooth skin and an upright appearance.

Full of seething, wormy, hollow feelings
rather nasty –
How beastly the bourgeois is!

Standing in their thousands, these appearances, in damp
    England
what a pity they can't all be kicked over
like sickening toadstools, and left to melt back, swiftly
into the soil of England.

The Oxford Voice

When you hear it languishing
and hooing and cooing and sidling through the front teeth
    the Oxford voice
      or worse still
   the would-be Oxford voice
you don't even laugh any more, you can't.

For every blooming bird is an Oxford cuckoo nowadays,
you can't sit on a bus nor in the tube
but it breathes gently and languishingly in the back of your
  neck.

And oh, so seductively superior, so seductively
    self-effacingly
    deprecatingly
     superior. –

We wouldn't insist on it for a moment
    but we are
     we are
    you admit we are
     superior. –

Leda

Come not with kisses
not with caresses
of hands and lips and murmurings;
come with a hiss of wings
and sea-touch tip of a beak
and treading of wet, webbed, wave-working feet
into the marsh-soft belly.

The Mosquito Knows

The mosquito knows full well, small as he is
he's a beast of prey.
But after all
he only takes his bellyful,
he doesn't put my blood in the bank.

Nottingham's New University

In Nottingham, that dismal town
where I went to school and college,
they've built a new university
for a new dispensation of knowledge.

Built it most grand and cakeily
out of the noble loot
derived from shrewd cash-chemistry
by good Sir Jesse Boot.

Little I thought, when I was a lad
and turned my modest penny
over on Boot's Cash Chemist's counter,
that Jesse, by turning many

millions of similar honest pence
over, would make a pile
that would rise at last and blossom out
in grand and cakey style

into a university
where smart men would dispense
doses of smart cash-chemistry
in language of common-sense!

That future Nottingham lads would be
cash-chemically B.Sc.
that Nottingham lights would rise and say:
– By Boots I am M.A.

From this I learn, though I knew it before
that culture has her roots
in the deep dung of cash, and lore
is a last offshoot of Boots.

Red-Herring

My father was a working man
   and a collier was he,
at six in the morning they turned him down
   and they turned him up for tea.

My mother was a superior soul
   a superior soul was she,
cut out to play a superior rôle
   in the god-damn bourgeoisie.

We children were the in-betweens
   little non-descripts were we,
indoors we called each other *you*,
   outside, it was *tha* and *thee*.

But time has fled, our parents are dead
   we've risen in the world all three;
but still we are in-betweens, we tread
   between the devil and the deep cold sea.

O I am a member of the bourgeoisie
   and a servant-maid brings me my tea –
But I'm always longing for someone to say:
   'ark 'ere, lad! atween thee an' me

they're a' a b—d —lot o' —s,
   an' I reckon it's nowt but right
we should start an' kick their —ses for 'em
   an' tell 'em to —.

Desire Is Dead

Desire may be dead
and still a man can be
a meeting place for sun and rain,
wonder outwaiting pain
as in a wintry tree.

Grasshopper Is a Burden

Desire has failed, desire has failed
and the critical grasshopper
has come down on the heart in a burden of locusts
and stripped it bare.

Innocent England

Oh what a pity, Oh! don't you agree
that figs aren't found in the land of the free!

Fig-trees don't grow in my native land;
there's never a fig-leaf near at hand

when you want one; so I did without;
and that is what the row's about.

Virginal, pure policemen came
and hid their faces for very shame,

while they carried the shameless things away
to gaol, to be hid from the light of day.

And Mr Mead, that old, old lily
said: 'Gross! coarse! hideous!' – and I, like a silly,

thought he meant the faces of the police-court officials,
and how right he was, and I signed my initials

to confirm what he said; but alas, he meant
my pictures, and on the proceedings went.

The upshot was, my picture must burn
that English artists might finally learn

when they painted a nude, to put a *cache sexe* on,
a cache sexe, a cache sexe, or else begone!

A fig-leaf; or, if you cannot find it
a wreath of mist, with nothing behind it.

A wreath of mist is the usual thing
in the north, to hide where the turtles sing.

Though they never sing, they never sing,
don't you dare to suggest such a thing

or Mr Mead will be after you.
– But what a pity I never knew

A wreath of English mist would do
as a cache sexe! I'd have put a whole fog.

But once and forever barks the old dog,
so my pictures are in prison, instead of in the Zoo.

Image-Making Love

And now
the best of all
is to be alone, to possess one's soul in silence.

Nakedly to be alone, unseen
is better than anything else in the world,
a relief like death.

Always
at the core of me
burns the small flame of anger, gnawing
from trespassed contacts, from red-hot finger bruises, on my
    inward flesh,
from hot, digging-in fingers of love.

Always
in the eyes of those who loved me
I have seen at last the image of him they loved
and took for me
mistook for me.

And always
it was a simulacrum, something
like me, and like a gibe at me.

So now I want, above all things
to preserve my nakedness
from the gibe of image-making love.

Intimates

Don't you care for my love? she said bitterly.

I handed her the mirror, and said:
Please address these questions to the proper person!
Please make all requests to head-quarters!
In all matters of emotional importance
please approach the supreme authority direct!
So I handed her the mirror.

And she would have broken it over my head,
but she caught sight of her own reflection
and that held her spellbound for two seconds
while I fled.

Andraitx – Pomegranate Flowers

It is June, it is June
the pomegranates are in flower,
the peasants are bending cutting the bearded wheat.

The pomegranates are in flower
beside the high-road, past the deathly dust,
and even the sea is silent in the sun.

Short gasps of flame in the green of night, way off
the pomegranates are in flower,
small sharp red fires in the night of leaves.

And noon is suddenly dark, is lustrous, is silent and dark
men are unseen, beneath the shading hats;
only, from out the foliage of the secret loins
red flamelets here and there reveal
a man, a woman there.

There Are Too Many People

There are too many people on earth
insipid, unsalted, rabbity, endlessly hopping.
They nibble the face of the earth to a desert.

Bells

The Mohammedans say that the sound of bells
especially big ones, is obscene;

That hard clapper striking in a hard mouth
and resounding after with a long hiss of insistence
is obscene.

Yet bells call the Christians to God
especially clapper bells, hard tongues wagging in hard mouths,
metal hitting on metal, to enforce our attention . . .
and bring us to God.

The soft thudding of drums
of fingers or fists or soft-skinned sticks upon the stretched
   membrane of sound
sends summons in the old hollows of the sun.

And the accumulated splashing of a gong
where tissue plunges into bronze with wide wild circles of sound
and leaves off,
belongs to the bamboo thickets, and the drake in the air flying
   past.

And the sound of a blast through the sea-curved core of a shell
when a black priest blows on a conch,
and the dawn-cry from a minaret, God is Great,
and the calling of the old Red Indian high on the pueblo roof
whose voice flies on and on, calling like a swan
singing between the sun and the marsh,
on and on, like a dark-faced bird singing alone
singing to the men below, the fellow-tribesmen
who go by without pausing, soft-foot, without listening, yet
   who hear:
there are other ways of summons, crying: Listen! Listen!
   Come near!

Trees in the Garden

Ah in the thunder air
how still the trees are!

And the lime-tree, lovely and tall, every leaf silent
hardly looses even a last breath of perfume.

And the ghostly, creamy coloured little tree of leaves
white, ivory white among the rambling greens
how evanescent, variegated elder, she hesitates on the green
    grass
as if, in another moment, she would disappear
with all her grace of foam!

And the larch that is only a column, it goes up too tall to see:
and the balsam-pines that are blue with the grey-blue
    blueness of things from the sea,
and the young copper beech, its leaves red-rosy at the ends
how still they are together, they stand so still
in the thunder air, all strangers to one another
as the green grass glows upwards, strangers in the silent
    garden.

    Lichtental

Storm in the Black Forest

Now it is almost night, from the bronzey soft sky
jugfull after jugfull of pure white liquid fire, bright white
tipples over and spills down,
and is gone
and gold-bronze flutters bent through the thick upper air.

And as the electric liquid pours out, sometimes
a still brighter white snake wriggles among it, spilled
and tumbling wriggling down the sky:
and then the heavens cackle with uncouth sounds.

And the rain won't come, the rain refuses to come!

This is the electricity that man is supposed to have mastered
chained, subjugated to his use!
supposed to!

Butterfly

Butterfly, the wind blows sea-ward, strong beyond the garden
    wall!
Butterfly, why do you settle on my shoe, and sip the dirt on
    my shoe,
Lifting your veined wings, lifting them? big white butterfly!

Already it is October, and the wind blows strong to the sea
from the hills where snow must have fallen, the wind is
    polished with snow.
Here in the garden, with red geraniums, it is warm, it is warm
but the wind blows strong to sea-ward, white butterfly,
    content on my shoe!

Will you go, will you go from my warm house?
Will you climb on your big soft wings, black-dotted,
as up an invisible rainbow, an arch
till the wind slides you sheer from the arch-crest
and in a strange level fluttering you go out to sea-ward, white
    speck!

Farewell, farewell, lost soul!
you have melted in the crystalline distance,
it is enough! I saw you vanish into air.

Bavarian Gentians

Not every man has gentians in his house
in soft September, at slow, sad Michaelmas.

Bavarian gentians, big and dark, only dark
darkening the day-time, torch-like with the smoking blueness
    of Pluto's gloom,
ribbed and torch-like, with their blaze of darkness spread blue
down flattening into points, flattened under the sweep of
    white day
torch-flower of the blue-smoking darkness, Pluto's dark-blue
    daze,
black lamps from the halls of Dis, burning dark blue,
giving off darkness, blue darkness, as Demeter's pale lamps
    give off light,
lead me then, lead the way.

Reach me a gentian, give me a torch!
let me guide myself with the blue, forked torch of this flower
down the darker and darker stairs, where blue is darkened on
    blueness
even where Persephone goes, just now, from the frosted
    September
to the sightless realm where darkness is awake upon the dark
and Persephone herself is but a voice
or a darkness invisible enfolded in the deeper dark
of the arms Plutonic, and pierced with the passion of dense
    gloom,
among the splendour of torches of darkness, shedding
    darkness on the lost bride and her groom.

The Ship of Death

I

Now it is autumn and the falling fruit
and the long journey towards oblivion.

The apples falling like great drops of dew
to bruise themselves an exit from themselves.

And it is time to go, to bid farewell
to one's own self, and find an exit
from the fallen self.

II

Have you built your ship of death, O have you?
O build your ship of death, for you will need it.

The grim frost is at hand, when the apples will fall
thick, almost thundrous, on the hardened earth.

And death is on the air like a smell of ashes!
Ah! can't you smell it?

And in the bruised body, the frightened soul
finds itself shrinking, wincing from the cold
that blows upon it through the orifices.

III

And can a man his own quietus make
with a bare bodkin?

With daggers, bodkins, bullets, man can make
a bruise or break of exit for his life;
but is that a quietus, O tell me, is it quietus?

Surely not so! for how could murder, even self-murder
ever a quietus make?

IV

O let us talk of quiet that we know,
that we can know, the deep and lovely quiet
of a strong heart at peace!

How can we this, our own quietus, make?

V

Build then the ship of death, for you must take
the longest journey, to oblivion.
And die the death, the long and painful death
that lies between the old self and the new.

Already our bodies are fallen, bruised, badly bruised,
already our souls are oozing through the exit
of the cruel bruise.

Already the dark and endless ocean of the end
is washing in through the breaches of our wounds,
already the flood is upon us.

Oh build your ship of death, your little ark
and furnish it with food, with little cakes, and wine
for the dark flight down oblivion.

VI

Piecemeal the body dies, and the timid soul
has her footing washed away, as the dark flood rises.

We are dying, we are dying, we are all of us dying
and nothing will stay the death-flood rising within us
and soon it will rise on the world, on the outside world.

We are dying, we are dying, piecemeal our bodies are dying
and our strength leaves us,
and our soul cowers naked in the dark rain over the flood,
cowering in the last branches of the tree of our life.

VII

We are dying, we are dying, so all we can do
is now to be willing to die, and to build the ship
of death to carry the soul on the longest journey.

A little ship, with oars and food
and little dishes, and all accoutrements
fitting and ready for the departing soul.

Now launch the small ship, now as the body dies
and life departs, launch out, the fragile soul
in the fragile ship of courage, the ark of faith
with its store of food and little cooking pans
and change of clothes,
upon the flood's black waste
upon the waters of the end
upon the sea of death, where still we sail
darkly, for we cannot steer, and have no port.

There is no port, there is nowhere to go
only the deepening black darkening still
blacker upon the soundless, ungurgling flood
darkness at one with darkness, up and down
and sideways utterly dark, so there is no direction
   any more.
And the little ship is there; yet she is gone.
She is not seen, for there is nothing to see her by.
She is gone! gone! and yet
somewhere she is there.
Nowhere!

VIII

And everything is gone, the body is gone
completely under, gone, entirely gone.
The upper darkness is heavy on the lower,
between them the little ship

is gone
she is gone.

It is the end, it is oblivion.

IX

And yet out of eternity, a thread
separates itself on the blackness,
a horizontal thread
that fumes a little with pallor upon the dark.

Is it illusion? or does the pallor fume
A little higher?
Ah wait, wait, for there's the dawn,
the cruel dawn of coming back to life
out of oblivion.

Wait, wait, the little ship
drifting, beneath the deathly ashy grey
of a flood-dawn.

Wait, wait! even so, a flush of yellow
and strangely, O chilled wan soul, a flush of rose.

A flush of rose, and the whole thing starts again.

X

The flood subsides, and the body, like a worn sea-shell
emerges strange and lovely.
And the little ship wings home, faltering and lapsing
on the pink flood,
and the frail soul steps out, into her house again
filling the heart with peace.

Swings the heart renewed with peace
even of oblivion.

Oh build your ship of death, oh build it!
for you will need it.
For the voyage of oblivion awaits you.

Eagle in New Mexico

On a low cedar-bush
In the flocculent ash of the sage-grey desert,
Ignoring our motor-car, black and always hurrying,
Hurrying,
Sits an eagle, erect and scorch-breasted;
From the top of a dark-haired cedar-bush
Issuing like a great cloven candle-flame
With its own alien aura.

Towards the sun, to south-west
A scorched breast, sun-turned forever.
A scorched breast breasting the blaze.
The sun-blaze of the desert.

Eagle, in the scorch forever,
Eagle, south-westward facing
Eagle, with the sickle dripping darkly above;

Can you still ignore it?
Can you ignore our passing in this machine?

Eagle, scorched-pallid out of the hair of the cedar,
Erect, with the God-thrust entering from below:
Eagle, gloved in feathers;
Oh soldier-erect big bird
In scorched white feathers
In burnt dark feathers
In feathers still fire-rusted;
Sickle-overswept, sickle dripping over and above.

Sunbreaster
Staring two ways at once, to right and left;
Masked-one,
Dark-wedged
Sickle-masked

With iron between your two eyes,
You feather-gloved
Down to the feet,
You foot-flint
Erect one,
With the God-thrust thrusting you silent from below.

You only stare at the sun with the one broad eye of your
    breast.
With your face, you face him with a rock,
A wedge,
The weapon of your face.

Oh yes, you face the sun
With a dagger of dark, live iron
That's been whetted and whetted in blood.

The dark cleaves down and weapon-hard downwards
    curving;
The dark drips down suspended
At the sun of your breast
Like a down-curved sword of Damocles,
Beaked eagle.

The God-thrust thrusting you silent and dark from
    beneath.
From where?
From the red-fibred bough of the cedar, from the cedar-roots,
    from the earth,
From the dark earth over the rock, from the dark rock over
    the fire,
    from the fire that boils in the molten heart of the world.

The heart of the world is the heart of the earth where a fire
    that is living throbs
Throb, throb, throb
And throws up strength that is living strength and regal into
    the feet;

Into the roots of the cedar, into the cedar-boughs,
And up the iron feet of the eagle in thrills of fiery power.

Lifts him fanning in the high empyrean
Where he stares at the sun.

Feather-ankles,
Fierce-foot,
Eagle, with Egyptian darkness jutting in front of your face;
Old one, erect on a bush,
Do you see the gold sun fluttering buoyantly in heaven
Like a boy in a meadow playing,
And his father watching him?

Are you the father-bird?
And is the sun your first-born, Only-begotten?
The gold sun shines in heaven only because he's allowed.
The old Father of life at the heart of the world, life-fire at the
    middle of the earth, this earth
Sent out the sun so that something should flutter in heaven;
And sent the eagle to keep an eye on him.

Erect, scorched-pallid out of the hair of the cedar,
All sickle-overswept, sickle dripping over and above,
Soldier-erect from the God-thrust, eagle
        with tearless eyes,
You who came before rock was smitten into weeping,
Dark-masked-one, day-starer, threatening the sun with your
    beak
Silent upon the American cedar-bush,
Threatener!

Will you take off your threat?
Or will you fulfil it?
Will you strike at the heart of the sun with your blood-welded
    beak?
Will you strike the sun's heart out again?
Will you? like an Aztec sacrifice reversed.

Oh vindictive eagle of America!
Oh sinister Indian eagle!
Oh eagle of kings and emperors!
What next?

Campions

The unclouded seas of bluebells have ebbed and passed
And the pale stars of forget-me-nots have climbed to the last
Rung of their life-ladders' fragile heights.
Now the trees with interlocked hands and arms uplifted hold
    back the light.

Though the purple dreams of the innocent spring have gone
And the glimmering dreamlets of the morning are pallid and
    wan
Though the year is ripening like a woman who has conceived
And the wood, like a manly husband, spreads softness and
    silence, thick-leaved:

The Campions drift in fragile, rosy mist,
Draw nearer, redden and laugh like young girls kissed
Into a daring, short-breath'd confession
Which opens earth and Heaven to Love's fugitive, glowing
    progression

Love-fire is drifting, though the bugle is prim and demure,
Love-light is glowing, though the guelder-rose is too chaste
    and pure
Ever to suffer love's wild attack,
For with the redness of laughter the battle is waging in the
    Campions' rosy wrack.

Guelder Roses

The guelder rose-bush is hung with coronets
Gently issuing from the massèd green;
Pale dreamy chaplets; a grey nun-sister sets
Such on the virgin hair of dead sixteen.

Chaplets of cream and distant green
That impress me like the thought-drenched eyes
Of some Pre-Raphaelite mystic queen
Who haunts me – with her lies.

Such pearled zones of fair sterility
Girdling with jewels the meanness of common things
Preaching in sad-moving silence a heart-hungry purity
In a day they are lost in the nothingness purity brings.

[At the end of a sweet spring day they will vanish;
Eloquent purity voiceless in the dust;
Utterly dead; who lived but to banish
The quick, kindling spark of a generous trust.

In the autumn I'll look for immortal fruit,
Heavy nodding clusters of crimson red,
Not on the stems of virginity, lovely and mute
But of those life-loving, careless of their rank among the
    dead.]

At the end of the sweet spring day they are gone
Forgotten, like last year's linnet song:
They were the halo, the eloquence – now is none
Left of their light, among the mean flowers' throng.

In the garnering autumn a glow of immortal fruit
– Heavy hanging clusters of crimson red
Swings round the stems of the many, insignificant mute
Life lovers, who could hope for no rank among the pallid
    dead.

Poetry of the Present

It seems when we hear a skylark singing as if sound were running forward into the future, running so fast and utterly without consideration, straight on into futurity. And when we hear a nightingale, we hear the pause and the rich, piercing rhythm of recollection, the perfected past. The lark may sound sad, but with the lovely lapsing sadness that is almost a swoon of hope. The nightingale's triumph is a pæan, but a death-pæan.

So it is with poetry. Poetry is, as a rule, either the voice of the far future, exquisite and ethereal, or it is the voice of the past, rich, magnificent. When the Greeks heard the *Iliad* and the *Odyssey*, they heard their own past calling in their hearts, as men far inland sometimes hear the sea and fall weak with powerful, wonderful regret, nostalgia; or else their own future rippled its time-beats through their blood, as they followed the painful, glamorous progress of the Ithacan. This was Homer to the Greeks: their Past, splendid with battles won and death achieved, and their Future, the magic wandering of Ulysses through the unknown.

With us it is the same. Our birds sing on the horizons. They sing out of the blue, beyond us, or out of the quenched night. They sing at dawn and sunset. Only the poor, shrill, tame canaries whistle while we talk. The wild birds begin before we are awake, or as we drop into dimness out of waking. Our poets sit by the gateways, some by the east, some by the west. As we arrive and as we go out our hearts surge with response. But whilst we are in the midst of life, we do not hear them.

The poetry of the beginning and the poetry of the end must have that exquisite finality, perfection which belongs to all that is far off. It is in the realm of all that is perfect. It is of the nature of all that is complete and consummate. This completeness, this consummateness, the finality and the perfection are conveyed in exquisite form: the perfect symmetry, the rhythm which returns upon itself like a dance where the hands link and loosen and link for the supreme moment of the end. Perfected bygone moments, perfected moments in the glimmering futurity, these are the treasured gem-like lyrics of Shelley and Keats.

But there is another kind of poetry: the poetry of that which is at hand: the immediate present. In the immediate present there is no perfection, no consummation, nothing finished. The strands are all flying, quivering, intermingling into the web, the waters are shaking the moon. There is no round, consummate moon on the face of running water, nor on the face of the unfinished tide. There are no gems of the living plasm. The living plasm vibrates unspeakably, it inhales the future, it exhales the past, it is the quick of both, and yet it is neither. There is no plasmic finality, nothing crystal, permanent. If we try to fix the living tissue, as the biologists fix it with formalin, we have only a hardened bit of the past, the bygone life under our observation.

Life, the ever-present, knows no finality, no finished crystallisation. The perfect rose is only a running flame, emerging and flowing off, and never in any sense at rest, static, finished. Herein lies its transcendent loveliness. The whole tide of all life and all time suddenly heaves, and appears before us as an apparition, a revelation. We look at the very white quick of nascent creation. A water-lily heaves herself from the flood, looks round, gleams, and is gone. We have seen the incarnation, the quick of the ever-swirling flood. We have seen the invisible. We have seen, we have touched, we have partaken of the very substance of creative change, creative mutation. If you tell me about the lotus, tell me of nothing changeless or eternal. Tell me of the mystery of the inexhaustible, forever-unfolding creative spark. Tell me of the incarnate disclosure of the flux, mutation in blossom, laughter and decay perfectly open in their transit, nude in their movement before us.

Let me feel the mud and the heavens in my lotus. Let me feel the heavy, silting, sucking mud, the spinning of sky winds. Let me feel them both in purest contact, the nakedness of sucking weight, nakedly passing radiance. Give me nothing fixed, set, static. Don't give me the infinite or the eternal: nothing of infinity, nothing of eternity. Give me the still, white seething, the incandescence and the coldness of the incarnate moment: the moment, the quick of all change and haste and opposition: the moment, the immediate present, the Now. The immediate moment is not a drop of water running downstream. It is the source and issue, the bubbling up of the stream. Here, in this very instant moment, up bubbles the stream of time, out of the wells of futurity, flowing on to the oceans of the past. The source, the issue, the creative quick.

There is poetry of this immediate present, instant poetry, as well as poetry of the infinite past and the infinite future. The seething poetry of the incarnate Now is supreme, beyond even the everlasting gems of the before and after. In its quivering momentaneity it surpasses the crystalline, pearl-hard jewels, the poems of the eternities. Do not ask for the qualities of the unfading timeless gems. Ask for the whiteness which is the seethe of mud, ask for that incipient putrescence which is the skies falling, ask for the never-pausing, never-ceasing life itself. There must be mutation, swifter than iridescence, haste, not rest, come-and-go, not fixity, inconclusiveness, immediacy, the quality of life itself, without dénouement or close. There must be the rapid momentaneous association of things which meet and pass on the forever incalculable journey of creation: everything left in its own rapid, fluid relationship with the rest of things.

This is the unrestful, ungraspable poetry of the sheer present, poetry whose very permanency lies in its wind-like transit. Whitman's is the best poetry of this kind. Without beginning and without end, without any base and pediment, it sweeps past for ever, like a wind that is forever in passage, and unchainable. Whitman truly looked before and after. But he did not sigh for what is not. The clue to all his utterance lies in the sheer appreciation of the instant moment, life surging itself into utterance at its very well-head. Eternity is only an abstraction from the actual present. Infinity is only a great reservoir of recollection, or a reservoir of aspiration: man-made. The quivering nimble hour of the present, this is the quick of Time. This is the immanence. The quick of the universe is the *pulsating, carnal self*, mysterious and palpable. So it is always.

Because Whitman put this into his poetry, we fear him and respect him so profoundly. We should not fear him if he sang only of the 'old unhappy far-off things', or of the 'wings of the morning'. It is because his heart beats with the urgent, insurgent Now, which is even upon us all, that we dread him. He is so near the quick.

From the foregoing it is obvious that the poetry of the instant present cannot have the same body or the same motion as the poetry of the before and after. It can never submit to the same conditions. It is never finished. There is no rhythm which returns upon itself, no serpent of eternity with its tail in its own mouth. There is no static perfection, none of that finality which we find so satisfying because we are so frightened.

Much has been written about free verse. But all that can be said, first and last, is that free verse is, or should be, direct utterance from the instant, whole man. It is the soul and the mind and body surging at once, nothing left out. They speak all together. There is some confusion, some discord. But the confusion and the discord only belong to the reality as noise belongs to the plunge of water. It is no use inventing fancy laws for free verse, no use drawing a melodic line which all the feet must toe. Free verse toes no melodic line, no matter what drill-sergeant. Whitman pruned away his clichés – perhaps his clichés of rhythm as well as of phrase. And this is about all we can do, deliberately, with free verse. We can get rid of the stereotyped movements and the old hackneyed associations of sound or sense. We can break down those artificial conduits and canals through which we do so love to force our utterance. We can break the stiff neck of habit. We can be in ourselves spontaneous and flexible as flame, we can see that utterance rushes out without artificial foam or artificial smoothness. But we cannot positively prescribe any motion, any rhythm. All the laws we invent or discover – it amounts to pretty much the same – will fail to apply to free verse. They will only apply to some form of restricted, limited unfree verse.

All we can say is that free verse does *not* have the same nature as restricted verse. It is not of the nature of reminiscence. It is not the past which we treasure in its perfection between our hands. Neither is it the crystal of the perfect future, into which we gaze. Its tide is neither the full, yearning flow of aspiration, nor the sweet, poignant ebb of remembrance and regret. The past and the future are the two great bournes of human emotion, the two great homes of the human days, the two eternities. They are both conclusive, final. Their beauty is the beauty of the goal, finished, perfected. Finished beauty and measured symmetry belong to the stable, unchanging eternities.

But in free verse we look for the insurgent naked throb of the instant moment. To break the lovely form of metrical verse, and to dish up the fragments as a new substance, called *vers libre*, this is what most of the free-versifiers accomplish. They do not know that free verse has its own *nature*, that it is neither star nor pearl, but instantaneous like plasm. It has no goal in either eternity. It has no finish. It has no satisfying stability, satisfying to those who like the immutable. None of this. It is the instant; the quick; the very jetting source of all will-be and has-been. The utterance is like a spasm, naked contact with all influences at once. It does not want to get anywhere. It just takes place.

For such utterance any externally-applied law would be mere shackles and death. The law must come new each time from within. The bird is on the wing in the winds, flexible to every breath, a living spark in the storm, its very flickering depending upon its supreme mutability and power of change. Whence such a bird came: whither it goes: from what solid earth it rose up, and upon what solid earth it will close its wings and settle, this is not the question. This is a question of before and after. Now, *now*, the bird is on the wing in the winds.

Such is the rare new poetry. One realm we have never conquered: the pure present. One great mystery of time is terra incognita to us: the instant. The most superb mystery we have hardly recognised: the immediate, instant self. The quick of all time is the instant. The quick of all the universe, of all creation, is the incarnate, carnal self. Poetry gave us the clue: free verse: Whitman. Now we know.

The ideal – what is the ideal? A figment. An abstraction. A static abstraction, abstracted from life. It is a fragment of the before or the after. It is a crystallised aspiration, or a crystallised remembrance: crystallised, set, finished. It is a thing set apart, in the great storehouse of eternity, the storehouse of finished things.

We do not speak of things crystallised and set apart. We speak of the instant, the immediate self, the very plasm of the self. We speak also of free verse.

All this should have come as a preface to *Look! We Have Come Through*! But is it not better to publish a preface long after the book it belongs to has appeared? For then the reader will have had his fair chance with the book, alone.